John Francis Fitzgerald (1863-1950) m. 1889 Mary Josephine Hannon (1865-1964)

Eunice Mary Kennedy (1921-)

Patricia Kennedy (1924-)

Robert Francis Kennedy (1925-1968)

Jean Ann Kennedy (1928-)

Edward Moore Kennedy (1932-)

PARTIAL KENNEDY FAMILY TREE

This partial Kennedy family tree focuses on the generation of John F. Kennedy and his siblings, going back to his grandparents and great-grandparents. Although it shows his marriage and children, it does not show the marriages and children of his brothers and sisters. All but Joe Jr. and Rosemary married. By 1972, when their families were complete, Rose Kennedy had twenty-nine grandchildren, most of whom would go on to marry and have families of their own.

JACK

JACK

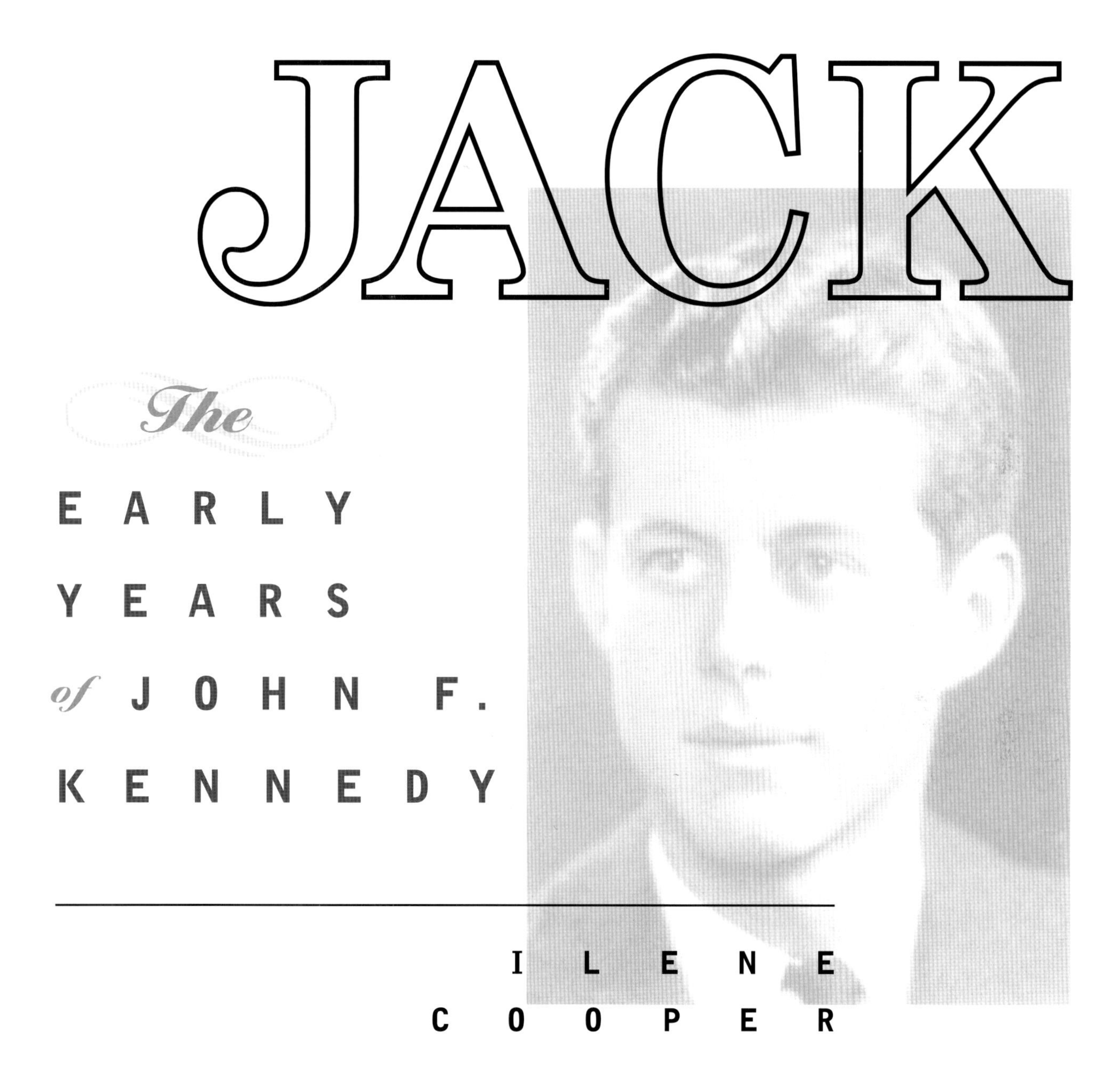

The EARLY YEARS *of* JOHN F. KENNEDY

ILENE COOPER

DUTTON CHILDREN'S BOOKS
NEW YORK

Library of Congress Cataloging-in-Publication Data
Cooper, Ilene.
Jack: the early years of John F. Kennedy / by Ilene Cooper.—1st ed.
p. cm.
Summary: A description of the childhood and youth of
John Fitzgerald Kennedy, the thirty-fifth president of the United States.
ISBN 0-525-46923-0
1. Kennedy, John F. (John Fitzgerald), 1917–1963—Childhood and youth—Juvenile literature. 2. Presidents—United States—Biography—Juvenile literature. [1. Kennedy, John F. (John Fitzgerald), 1917–1963—Childhood and youth. 2. Presidents.] I. Title.
E842.Z9 C66 2003 973.922'092—dc21 [B] 2002075912

Published in the United States by Dutton Children's Books,
a division of Penguin Putnam Books for Young Readers
345 Hudson Street, New York, New York 10014
www.penguinputnam.com

Designed by Heather Wood

Printed in China
First Edition
1 2 3 4 5 6 7 8 9 10

PHOTO CREDITS

pages ii, 47, 140: © Bachrach/John F. Kennedy Library;
page 66: © *The Boston Globe*; pages 6, 84, 95: John F. Kennedy Library Foundation;
pages 11, 14, 15: Courtesy National Park Service, John F. Kennedy National Historic Site;
page 80: Royal Atelier/John F. Kennedy Library; page 149: Cecil Stoughton, White House/John F. Kennedy Library.
All other photos in the text appear courtesy of the John F. Kennedy Library.

FOR SYLVIA, WHO TOOK ME ALL OVER MASSACHUSETTS,
AND BILL, WHO TAKES ME EVERYWHERE ELSE

Special thanks to Donna Brooks for all the time, effort, and care she put into this book. Thank you to Margaret Woollatt, Hazel Rochman, and John Green for their careful readings of this manuscript in its many and varied stages. And thanks to Liz Graves, Heather Wood, and Rosanne Lauer, of Dutton Children's Books, and to the staff of the John F. Kennedy Library, especially photo archivist James Hill, who offered so much help.

CONTENTS

THE DARE 3

CHAPTER I
"A VERY, VERY SICK LITTLE BOY" 5

CHAPTER II
"WE WANT WINNERS" 13

CHAPTER III
"BETTER TO TAKE IT IN STRIDE" 28

CHAPTER IV
"WEAVING DAYDREAMS" 43

CHAPTER V
"A REAL STIGMA" 53

CHAPTER VI
HYANNIS PORT AND HOLLYWOOD 63

CHAPTER VII

"THE BOY WHO DOESN'T GET THINGS DONE" *79*

CHAPTER VIII

HOMESICK *88*

CHAPTER IX

"QUITE DIFFERENT FROM JOE" *97*

CHAPTER X

JACK AND LEM *109*

CHAPTER XI

"AN INNER EYE" *118*

CHAPTER XII

MUCKERS *128*

AFTERWORD *139*

SOURCE NOTES *155*

BIBLIOGRAPHY *163*

INDEX *165*

JACK

THE DARE

The dare was simple. Jack listened as his brother Joe proposed a bicycle race around the block. The boys would pedal off in opposite directions, and when they met up again, whoever swerved first would be a chicken. Joe, older, bigger, and stronger, was sure that it would be Jack. Jack, almost two years younger, scrawny yet scrappy, was determined not to give Joe the satisfaction.

Ready, set . . . they sped away from each other. Faster and faster they pedaled. As they raced around the corner, legs pumping, neither boy would yield.

Smash! With force and fury, they crashed together. Joe came away unhurt. Jack flew off his bike and fell to the pavement, a bloody mess. At the hospital, it took twenty-eight stitches to sew him back together.

Jack Kennedy remembered this encounter all his life.

In the Kennedy household, winning was all-important. The boys' father insisted he wanted winners in the house, not losers. To young Jack, it seemed as if Joe was the older brother who would always triumph—the one who would walk away without a scratch. Jack was the second son, and coming in second seemed to be his lot in life.

All through his growing-up years, Jack wondered if he should struggle against his place in the family or give in to it. Keep pedaling or swerve out of the way? He had other questions, too. As a Kennedy, Jack was a child of wealth and privilege. But he was also raised with pressures and expectations: follow the rules, work hard, succeed. How could he make a place for himself in his family—and the larger world—when often he didn't do any of those things?

Jack Kennedy's life was a gift, but one that was wrapped with many strings. He spent much of his early years trying to untangle them.

"A VERY, VERY SICK LITTLE BOY"

CHAPTER I

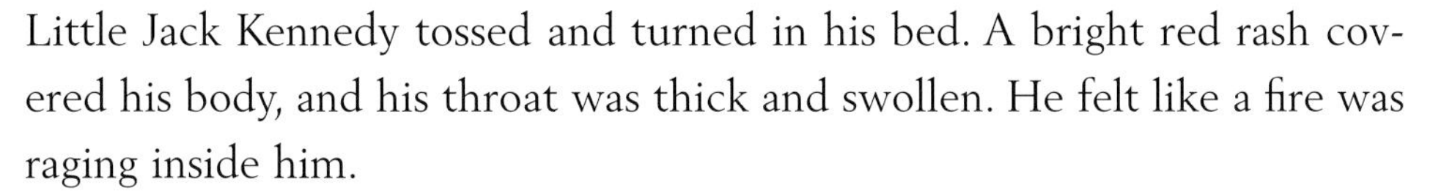

Little Jack Kennedy tossed and turned in his bed. A bright red rash covered his body, and his throat was thick and swollen. He felt like a fire was raging inside him.

He heard adults whisper "scarlet fever." But he was only two and a half, so he didn't know what the words meant. His parents knew all too well. In the late winter of 1920 when Jack became ill, there were not yet medications like penicillin to fight the disease. For children, scarlet fever often meant death.

The local Board of Health issued regulations about what to do if this very contagious disease struck a household. First, a card had to go up on the front and back doors stating that there was scarlet fever in the home. The patient had to be isolated for at least five weeks. Dirty clothes could not be sent to the laundry, and even library books touched by the patient had to be disinfected. The house, too, had to be disinfected after the patient recovered—or died.

Since young children were at special risk for catching scarlet fever,

THE EARLY YEARS

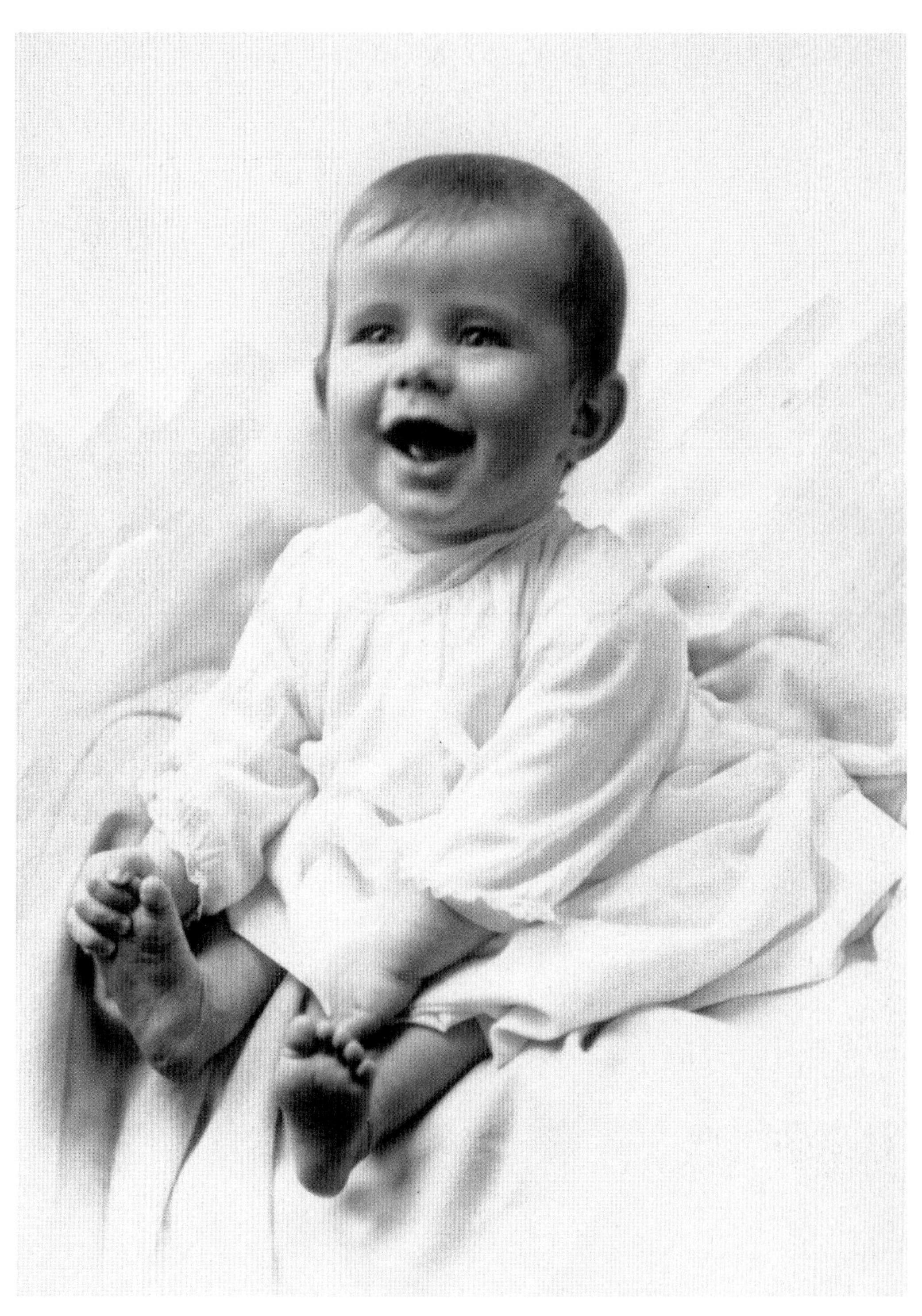

A happy baby, John Fitzgerald Kennedy in his first formal photograph

Jack's brother, four-year-old Joe Jr., and his sister Rosemary, fifteen months old, were kept away from him. They had to be isolated from the outside world as well, in case they were already infected with the illness and able to carry it to others.

Worse for Jack, his mother couldn't comfort him or even give him a hug. Lying exhausted in a nearby bedroom, Rose Kennedy had given birth to her fourth child, Kathleen, only hours after Jack's symptoms had appeared. The weakened Mrs. Kennedy and the newborn baby were highly susceptible to scarlet fever. In any case, Rose was in no shape to care for a seriously ill child. No wonder Mrs. Kennedy later said that Jack's illness threw the household into a state of "frantic terror."

So Jack lay listless and miserable, missing his mother, as his fever climbed to 104 degrees. His Irish nanny, Kico Conboy, tried to distract him with stories about wily leprechauns and the fairy folk who romped

A charming portrait of Rose Kennedy and her three oldest children, Joe Jr., Jack, and baby Rosemary. The next year, a few hours before the birth of his sister Kathleen, Jack would come down with scarlet fever.

through the Irish countryside. Usually Jack loved those stories, but now he was too ill to pay attention. Sometimes he looked over at his toys waiting to be played with or at the set of metal train cars sitting silently on their small track. But most of the time he just clutched his favorite teddy bear and drifted in and out of sleep.

Meanwhile, his father, Joseph P. Kennedy, a dynamic but controlling man, was trying desperately to find some special medical help for Jack, something more than the family doctor could offer. He was also concerned for the rest of his household; they'd all be safer if Jack was in the hospital. Unfortunately, Brookline, Massachusetts, the suburb of Boston where the Kennedys lived, had no facility with space for patients with contagious diseases. A special ward existed in the Boston City Hospital, which had an excellent reputation for dealing with epidemics like scarlet fever. But that ward had only 125 beds, and those were supposed to be just for Boston residents.

Luckily for young Jack, his family had connections that the other six hundred children ill in Boston during this epidemic of scarlet fever did not. Jack, christened John Fitzgerald Kennedy, had been named for his mother's father, John Fitzgerald, who was a beloved former mayor of Boston. Thanks to Grandpa Fitzgerald's influence, the Boston City Hospital made room for Jack.

Still, getting into the hospital was no guarantee that Jack would recover. No matter what the doctors tried, for several weeks his temperature hovered around 102. As his mother put it later, he was a "very, very sick little boy." From his bed in an isolation ward, Jack watched as unfamiliar doctors and nurses wearing masks came and went in his room, their hospital gowns reeking of disinfectant. Jack must have been frightened and upset by the strange sights and smells, and lonely for home.

His helpless parents tried to cope as best they could. A worried Rose Kennedy recovered from Kathleen's birth and watched over her other children, even as her thoughts were at the hospital with Jack. She prayed hard, drawing on her Catholic faith for strength.

For Joseph Kennedy, Jack's illness was more than just terrifying—it made him rethink his priorities in life. A successful businessman, once the youngest bank president in the country, Mr. Kennedy loved his family. But his primary focus had always been on getting ahead in the world. Now, seeing his son lying so small and helpless in a hospital bed, Jack's father realized how devastated he would be if anything happened to one of his children.

For the first time in anyone's memory, Mr. Kennedy left work early each day. He sat at Jack's bedside, and perhaps he surprised even himself by promising God that if Jack lived, he would give half of his wealth to a Catholic charity.

In mid-March, almost a month after Jack had contracted scarlet fever, he began to feel better. His fever went down and his rash faded. Yet he was still a long way from well. He would spend almost another month in the hospital, but now that he was recovering, his playful side started to shine through. Although Jack Kennedy's future was to be filled with serious illness, he learned an important lesson early on: he could come through pain, fear, and isolation with his own vivacious personality intact.

Even at this young age, he drew people to him. His nurses were utterly charmed by the sandy-haired, blue-eyed little boy. Many children passed through their care, but the staff agreed that Jack was one patient they'd remember. "We all love him dearly," said one nurse. Another told Mr. Kennedy, "Jack is certainly the nicest little boy I have ever seen." When Jack was well enough to leave the hospital, he didn't go home. He was sent off with a private nurse to a rest home in woodsy Poland Springs, Maine, for two more weeks of recovery. There he could breathe the fresh, country air and build up his strength.

When Mr. Kennedy felt assured that Jack would recover, he wrote a check for $3,500 to the Guild of St. Apollonia, a group of Catholic doctors and dentists that provided free medical care to poor children. It was a hefty sum at a time when many people worked long and hard for a few dollars a week. Perhaps not hefty enough, however, to fulfill his promise

THE EARLY YEARS

Jack was an endearing toddler who drew people to him.

of donating half his wealth. Mr. Kennedy had a reputation for being a shrewd, if sometimes unscrupulous, businessman. Later some people thought he might have fudged a bit on the amount of his fortune, counting only the cash he had on hand, not all of his investments, when he came up with the figure of $3,500.

Jack's ordeal had started in February, when it was cold and raw outside. He arrived home in May as the flowers were bursting into bloom, just in time for his third birthday. Three months is a long time in the life of a three-year-old, especially one who is ill and far away from everything familiar. It must have been a happy homecoming for Jack at 83 Beals Street, in Brookline—yet a little strange, as well. He was meeting his baby sister, Kathleen, for the first time. And he was no longer the center of attention as he had been when he was ill. Now he was just one of several children again, and not even the most important. That position in the

83 Beals Street, Brookline, Massachusetts. Today Jack's first home is a National Historic Site.

family belonged to his brother, Joe Jr., almost five years old. Joe Jr. was the strong, sturdy child on whom his parents doted.

Today, the house on Beals Street is a National Historic Site, the birthplace of John Fitzgerald Kennedy, the thirty-fifth president of the United States. Restored with many pieces of the family's original furniture, it looks much the same as it did when the Kennedys lived there. Many people visit this public museum each year.

But long before anyone knew the heights to which Jack Kennedy would rise, the small, gray-shingled house was simply the place where on May 29, 1917, he was born—his first home, the scene of his earliest memories.

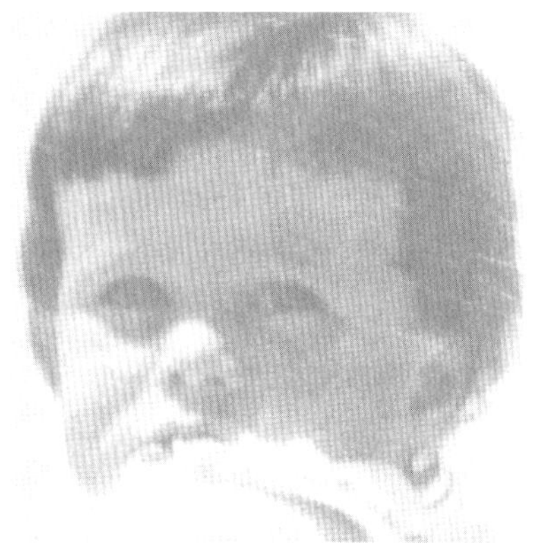

"WE WANT WINNERS"

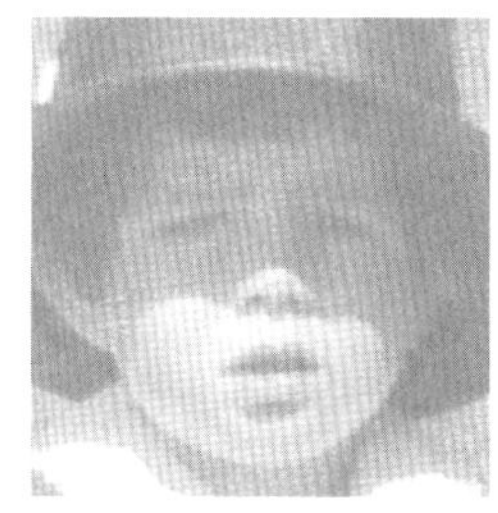

CHAPTER II

Jack was too young to know it, but he was lucky to spend his earliest years in a comfortable two-and-a-half-story house with a front porch and a backyard, both excellent spots to play.

In Boston, the bustling city a trolley-car ride away from Brookline, many people lived in dingy, dirty tenement houses so crowded that sixteen families sometimes shared one bathroom. The nicely furnished house on Beals Street, although compact, had a living room, dining room, and a kitchen downstairs, and three bedrooms upstairs. There were other signs of the Kennedy family's prosperity. The household boasted a live-in maid, who shared the attic bedroom with Kico, the children's nanny. For seven dollars a week, the maid did all the cleaning and washing. And while most people in and around Boston used public transportation, Mr. Kennedy was the proud owner of a black Model T Ford.

The Beals Street house offered Jack lots of opportunities for good times. The white-curtained bedroom he shared with Joe was small, but it had space for toys: wooden blocks, a small train, and a bookcase filled with volumes of fairy tales and nursery rhymes. In the living room, with its gas fireplace that kept the room toasty in winter, Jack scampered about on the Oriental carpet or sat on the overstuffed couch and listened to his mother sing and play her family's favorite songs on the baby grand piano, her most prized possession. Around a large, mahogany table in the dining room, the Kennedy family enjoyed festive events like Christmas dinner and birthday parties. Outside, Jack and Joe tusseled in the fenced-in yard, tossing leaves at each other in the autumn, cavorting in the summer sun, or making snowballs from the winter snow.

During the 1920s, the Kennedy family kept expanding—eventually there would be nine children in all—and so did the family wealth. Mr. Kennedy made his money in a variety of businesses. He had left Columbia Trust, the small bank over which he presided, during World War I.

The nursery at 83 Beals Street. The bassinet on wheels would eventually hold each of the nine Kennedy children.

That brutal, destructive conflict started in Europe in 1914 and pitted the Allies, which included Great Britain, France, Italy, and Russia, against Germany. The United States entered the war on the side of the Allies in 1917, a month before Jack was born. Instead of volunteering to serve in the armed forces, as most of his friends did, Joseph Kennedy took a job running a shipyard for the U.S. government.

The Fore River shipyard was an essential part of the effort to build destroyers and other vessels that America needed to counteract the threat of German submarines. Always the sharp businessman, Mr. Kennedy struck a deal with the management of the shipyard to keep the proceeds from the employees' cafeteria for himself. The shipyard, which built thirty-six destroyers in twenty-seven months, was like a town unto itself. Its cafeteria could feed fourteen hundred people at one time, so the profits were sizable.

After the war ended in 1918, Mr. Kennedy became a stockbroker, im-

The centerpiece of the living room was an Ivers & Pond piano given to Mr. and Mrs. Kennedy by her uncles as a wedding present. Rose hung reproductions of the paintings she had seen in European museums on the walls.

mersing himself in the stock market, where one could win—or lose—huge sums of money very quickly. Joe Kennedy made sure he was a winner.

While her husband was making his way in the world, Rose Kennedy was staying close to home. That had not always been the case. Before she was married, Rose had been the belle of Boston, serving as official hostess for her father, Mayor Fitzgerald, a job her own mother, a shy, reserved woman, didn't relish. Rose went to public events and private parties with him and hobnobbed with important people. She also had the advantage of having been educated abroad and having traveled in Holland, Ger-

Determined, focused, and forceful, Joseph P. Kennedy pursued success from an early age.

many, France, and England. Fluent in both French and German, she loved learning foreign languages.

Despite the worldly life she led, Rose Kennedy was raised to believe a woman's highest calling was to be a wife and mother. But now that she was both, she found herself chafing at the restrictions of her existence. Her husband was out building his fortune; she was tied to her house, trying to cope with the needs and demands of four children under the age of five.

For a time Mrs. Kennedy was unhappy, something she wasn't used to. After a good deal of prayer and reflection, she decided she would not fight her situation but transform it. Like her husband, she would be an executive—only instead of overseeing a business, she would be running a well-managed and efficient household.

First Mrs. Kennedy decided she needed a bigger home to accommodate the family, and Mr. Kennedy agreed. On the corner of Naples and Abbottsford Roads, a short walk from the Beals Street house, sat a large Victorian-style home with a spacious front porch. Round turret windows gave it the look of a castle.

In the fall of 1920, several months after Jack's recovery from scarlet fever, the family moved into the twelve-room house at 131 Naples Road. It was not only large enough for the Kennedys but could accommodate the additional servants they planned to hire, including a cook and a chauffeur.

Inside, the Kennedys filled the house with all the most modern conveniences, including a refrigerator, a washing machine, and a vacuum cleaner. Outside was a garage large

In 1906, a pretty and poised Rose Fitzgerald received her high school diploma from her father, the mayor of Boston. Only fifteen years old when she graduated from Dorchester High, Rose was the youngest graduate in the school's history.

enough for the Model T and for the Rolls-Royce that Mr. Kennedy would soon acquire.

Rose Kennedy put her energies into planning, organizing, and supervising her household. That meant making sure things ran on schedule, that meals were nutritious, and that the children looked clean and tidy. The more menial tasks, like changing diapers and washing bottles, were left to Kico and the maid. As her family grew, Mrs. Kennedy needed a way to keep track of all the details of her children's lives. She bought a file box and started making cards for each child, noting his or her vital statistics: birthdays, weights and heights, dates of baptisms and confirmations. The cards also contained running lists of their illnesses. Jack had most of these particular notations. He was born with a slightly deformed back, an easily upset stomach that made it hard for him to keep down milk, and he seemed to catch every childhood disease.

The Kennedy house at the corner of Abbottsford and Naples Roads in Brookline. Mrs. Kennedy put a folding gate at the entrance of the wraparound porch, making it a safe, fun place for the children to play.

Mrs. Kennedy believed that one way to keep the children healthy was to make sure they got plenty of fresh air, so she started taking them on daily walks. Looking back, she would remember how much time she spent in those days before Velcro or even zippers, buttoning and unbuttoning her children's clothes, an especially tiresome task in winter. But the walks were a way to get both herself and her children out of the house.

They made quite a little parade. Rose would push baby Kathleen in a buggy while Rosemary toddled along beside her. Jack and Joe walked or rode their tricycles. Jack, thin and wiry, with an infectious grin, liked saying hello to the policeman and the mailman, or to the neighbors they passed along the way. The destination was usually Coolidge Corner, the nearby shopping area. There, they would pop into the local variety store to pick up some household item or perhaps a small treat like lollipops. Often they would duck into St. Aiden's, the local Catholic church, for a prayer; church wasn't only for Sundays or holy days in Rose Kennedy's family.

It was very important to Mrs. Kennedy that her children be strong Roman Catholics. As soon as Jack and all the little Kennedys could form the words, she taught them the prayers of their religion. Jack got down on his knees and said his prayers each night before he went to bed and when he was old enough, he became an altar boy, assisting the priest at Mass. Besides visiting nearby St. Aiden's, with its rustic stone exterior, Mrs. Kennedy also took the children into Boston, where she had at-

Jack (left) and Joe decked out in the fashion of the day. Mrs. Kennedy often dressed the boys alike.

tended services as a girl, so they could be awed by the pomp and ceremony of the larger, grander churches.

Catholicism was Rose's way to center her family. Joe Sr.'s idea was to make sure the Kennedys felt themselves a strong unit that could close ranks against outsiders. Even though Mr. Kennedy was growing more successful and rich by the day, he knew what it was like to feel the sting of discrimination. The Kennedy family, and Rose's family, the Fitzgeralds, had originally come from Ireland, and the Irish were often looked down upon in Boston. The roots of this discrimination stretched all the way back to the "old country."

The Irish-Catholic immigrants who began arriving in Boston Harbor in the 1840s were mostly poor, uneducated farmers fleeing the potato famine that was starving their country. Not that these peasants actually owned the land they tilled. Since the seventeenth century Ireland had been under the control of the British. Irish farmers had to rent small plots in their own country from wealthy English people, the gentry, who owned the land but mostly lived across the sea, in England. The gentry didn't want to share power with the Irish-Catholic majority, refusing not only to let them own land, but also to vote, or even to attend school.

In 1845, Irish farmers started noticing a white fungus on their potatoes. It was a blight that killed the potatoes as they were growing in the ground. Weather conditions that year promoted the spread of the blight. Four successive crop failures later, the population was starving to death. A quarter of those who survived scraped together what money they could and left Ireland. Most people decided to immigrate to the United States.

Jack's great-grandparents, the Fitzgeralds and the Kennedys, left Ireland in the mid-nineteenth century. They sailed across the cold, rough Atlantic to Boston for a fare of about twenty dollars, but they didn't get much for their money. The journey was marked by filth, rats, rancid food, and rampant illness that caused many deaths en route. The Irish had a bitter nickname for their mode of transportation to the New World—"coffin ships."

Jack Kennedy's grandparents, P.J. Kennedy and his wife, Mary, flanked by relatives. Both P.J.'s and Mary's parents left Ireland during the Irish potato famine.

Nor was there a welcome waiting for those who survived the voyage to Boston. By 1860, the year Abraham Lincoln was elected president, Boston's population had almost doubled from twenty years earlier. The crush of immigrants turned large sections of the city into slums and tenements. Landlords gouged the Irish newcomers, making them pay high rents for tiny, crowded accommodations. Apartments might house five to fifteen people. In one apartment, the number climbed to thirty-nine.

The Irish had braved their difficult journey to start life over in a free country, but the prejudice and ill feelings between the Irish and British had crossed the Atlantic with them. Among Boston Protestants were families like the Lowells, the Cabots, and the Lodges, descendants of the powerful landowning gentry back in England. With wealth, social standing, and a pride in the contributions their families had made to America since colonial times, this exclusive group, often known as "the Bostonians," closed ranks and formed a tightly knit group.

These "first families" of Boston seemed to feel it was their God-given right to be society's elite and to look down on others. A popular ditty summed up their snobbery with rueful humor:

Here's to the city of Boston,
The home of the bean and the cod,
Where the Lodges speak only to Cabots,
And the Cabots talk only to God.

The Bostonians, with their inherited wealth and privilege, didn't intend to share their power with anyone else, especially not with the poor and often ill-educated Irish immigrants. As for the Irish, they felt that the descendants of those who had oppressed them in Ireland were now keeping them from achieving the prosperity and cultural status they were willing to work hard to attain. The prejudice spread beyond the boundaries of the highest levels of society. "Help Wanted" ads often read, NO IRISH NEED

APPLY. By the beginning of the twentieth century, however, the Bostonians were forced to share political power. There were so many voters of Irish descent living in Boston that they were able to elect Irish politicians—like Rose's father, John "Honey Fitz" Fitzgerald—into office.

Discrimination against those of Irish extraction infuriated Joe Kennedy. He considered himself an American success story. His father, Patrick Joseph Kennedy—P.J.—was born in the United States in 1857, nine years after his parents emigrated from Ireland. A part-time politician and a full-time saloon keeper, P.J. produced a life comfortable enough to push his family into the burgeoning Irish middle class. Joe was born in 1888. His ambitious mother, Mary, made sure he attended the well-regarded Boston Latin school. He was a good enough high school student and athlete to be accepted at Harvard University. Although the university was a favorite choice of monied and well-connected families, it was also trying to diversify its student population by admitting boys of more modest circumstances. With his friendly, outgoing personality, Joe was popular enough to hope that the upper-crust boys at Harvard would ask him to join their prestigious social clubs. They didn't, and it rankled. He was soon to learn that New England snobbery only began at school—it didn't end there. After their marriage, Joe and Rose were at the top of Irish-Catholic society. But as time went on and they built a family, it became clear that the old Bostonians, who considered Joe, especially, a social climber, would never accept them. The rejection made him determined to someday show this insular group that the Kennedys were a force to be reckoned with.

WANTED—A good, reliable woman to take the care of a boy two years old, in a small family in Brookline. Good wages and a permanent situation given. No washing or ironing will be required, but good recommendations as to character and capacity demanded. Postively no Irish need apply. Call at 224 Washington street, corner of Summer street.
6t jy 28

Irish immigrants had hopes of coming to a land of liberty, but many were met with prejudice. Newspaper ads often informed the newcomers not to bother applying for the advertised jobs.

Along with family togetherness and religious faith, Mr. and Mrs. Kennedy wanted to instill one more important idea in their children: to do their best at everything they attempted. Trying, however, wasn't good enough. Succeeding was what counted. As Mr. Kennedy often said, "We want winners in this house, not losers." Jack heard this refrain over and over from the time he was a little boy.

Both Joe and Rose thought that perhaps the best way to make their children winners was to shape their eldest, Joe Jr., into a model child whom all the younger ones would look up to and imitate. As Rose later explained, "If you bring up the eldest son right, the way you want the others to go, that is very important because the younger ones watch him. . . . If he works at his studies and his sports until he is praised, the others will follow his example." This philosophy was not always easy for Jack to live with, because it meant much of his parents' attention went to his brother Joe.

Luckily for Mr. and Mrs. Kennedy, young Joe was a willing bit of clay, ready to be molded. From his youngest days, Joe Jr. tried to be successful at everything he undertook, whether it was throwing a ball or doing his schoolwork. A handsome, appealing child who had his mother's dark blue eyes and his father's sandy hair, Joe Jr. seemed to understand from a very early age that he was to have the most special role among the Kennedy children. Comfortable in his position and a natural leader, he was a kind, helpful brother to his younger siblings—except when it came to Jack.

Many years later Jack described his brother as "a bit of a bully" and "pugnacious"—quarrelsome and combative. He admitted that Joe's overbearing personality "was a problem during my boyhood." Their rivalry played out at home, in school, and on the athletic field. During games of catch, Joe would throw the ball at Jack instead of to him, sometimes slamming Jack so hard, it knocked him down. Like many big brothers, Joe enjoyed having a younger brother to boss around, but Joe tried to impose his will with his fists just as often as with his words.

Joseph Kennedy holding his prized possessions—his namesake, Joe Kennedy Jr., on the left, and Jack, on the right

Yet if Joe knew how to push Jack, Jack came up with all sorts of ways to push right back.

A typical incident occurred at the family dinner table when the boys were young. Jack knew very well that his brother loved desserts and liked to savor them slowly. One night, Joe scraped the rich, gooey chocolate icing off his cake to save for later. Jack snuck the plate away and gobbled down the icing in front of Joe. Joe gave his brother a whack; Jack let out a yell and hit him back. Both boys got sent off to bed.

The brothers weren't always at each other's throats. Often they would play together and pull pranks. As youngsters, they mischievously marked up a restaurant sign that said NO DOGS ALLOWED by adding the word HOT in front of DOGS. Jack and Joe enjoyed singing a song about bedbugs and cooties and even started a club together. They initiated new members by sticking them with pins.

Despite the fun, Jack was always aware of the competition that colored every aspect of their relationship. Perhaps the boys were at odds because they were so close in age—only twenty-two months apart. Maybe it was the difference in their personalities—Jack was elfin and witty, Joe responsible and hardheaded. Or it might simply have been that everyone, from their parents to their siblings to the servants, regarded Joe as someone special, and Jack wanted a piece of that admiration for himself.

A steady Joe Jr. and an impish Jack, with sister Kathleen looking on

"BETTER TO TAKE IT IN STRIDE"

CHAPTER III

Jack Kennedy spent most of his boyhood during a fascinating time in American history: the decade of the 1920s. During and after World War I, the United States changed from a mostly rural society to an urban one. Some people moved from farms to the cities seeking job opportunities; others came for the excitement of city life. Many soldiers, fresh from their war experiences, wanted to make new starts in urban areas. One popular song described the lure of the city for soldiers who had experienced cosmopolitan places like Paris, France, while fighting overseas: "How 'Ya Gonna Keep 'Em Down on the Farm, After They've Seen Paree?"

The 1920s were nicknamed the "Roaring Twenties." The name captured the excitement of the era, but perhaps it also stood for all the new sounds that were being carried into people's lives through the radio, telephone, and the movies. Inventions such as these, and others like automobiles and washing machines, became more readily available to the average American during the Roaring Twenties.

The rumble of airplanes was another fresh sound. In 1927, Charles

Lindbergh made the first solo flight across the Atlantic, launching the age of modern aviation. This daring deed turned Lindbergh into a hero. The Roaring Twenties, which saw men and women making their marks in all sorts of new fields, seemed to encourage a new breed of fans eager to support people of outstanding accomplishment. Baseball's Babe Ruth and nineteen-year-old Gertrude Ederle, who became the first woman to swim the English Channel, were among those admired by the public.

The 1920s were not free of problems, of course. Racial troubles existed in both the North and the South. The influx of people into the cities sometimes caused a breakdown in family relationships and an increase in crime. Still, for most people this was a time of optimism, fueled by the booming post-war economy, in which Joseph P. Kennedy was participating fully.

Although the Kennedys certainly lived with the trappings of wealth, Mr. and Mrs. Kennedy were not overly indulgent. They wanted their chil-

Rose Kennedy said, "One of the great thrills of my life was the day my husband drove home in our very own, brand-new, gleaming black Model T Ford." Here, Joe Jr. and Jack stand on the running board with their father alongside.

dren to know that there were many simple pleasures available to everyone. So, they made sure Jack and his siblings had fun without spending a lot of money.

Boston winters provided plenty of snow for sledding and skating, two activities Jack enjoyed, though ice skates were much different in those days. Instead of pulling on shoe skates, Jack used a key to screw metal runners onto the soles of his regular shoes. Then, to secure the skates, he had to wrap leather straps around the shoes and his ankles. In this imperfect system, the straps would loosen and slide down, frequently needing to be re-bound. Jack soon found out that learning how to put on the skates was almost as hard as skating itself.

In July and August, when the weather turned hot, the family would spend time on the beaches along the Massachusetts coast. The water could be chilly, but the rolling waves and the sandy dunes, with their tall grasses blowing in the breeze, meant summer to the young Kennedys. It's easy to see Jack as a little boy dashing across the wet sand, leaving footprints in his wake, wrestling the waves in a small rowboat, and enjoying seaside picnics with delicious food like Boston cream pie, thick with custard in the middle and covered with chocolate on top.

When Jack and his brothers and sisters weren't playing in the sand or swimming in the ocean, Mrs. Kennedy liked to plan the occasional excursion; she was always looking for ways to enlighten her children as well as entertain them.

One day she decided that rather than just buying blueberries at the store, it would be more interesting for her five young ones—Joe, Jack, Rosemary, Kathleen, and Eunice (who had been born in 1921)—to see how the succulent berries grew wild on Cape Cod and to pick them for themselves. So Jack and the others were packed into the car, and Mrs. Kennedy drove until she found just what she was looking for—a large sunny blueberry patch in the middle of a field of colorful wildflowers.

As she remembered the incident, each child got a little pail. Jack sat on

Jack, around age six, dressed for Halloween as a Keystone Kop. The Kops were a slapstick gang of policemen who appeared in silent films.

the ground picking at the lower branches while the others picked berries from the middle and the top. All went well until Eunice let out a shriek. She had been stung by a bumblebee. A few minutes later Jack jumped up, yelling and waving his arms. He had been sitting on an anthill, and now there were ants crawling all over him.

"Get them off me!" In short order, Jack was out of his clothes, which had to be shaken and brushed free of the insects. But now all the other kids were fussing, thinking that they, too, might be stung by bees or find themselves covered with ants. Mrs. Kennedy decided that all in all it was easier to buy her blueberries at the store, and that was the end of the berry picking.

Eventually the Kennedys would buy a house in Hyannis Port, on Cape Cod. Before that, they spent their summers at several different Massachusetts beach towns. Joe Jr., a July baby, was born in Hull, located on a bay and home to Nantasket Beach, a pretty resort area. Dotted with sparkling lights, Nantasket at night was all aglow. Later, the family spent several summers in a rented house on Cohasset's untamed beach. Most

The Kennedy children enjoying some summer fun in Cohasset, Massachusetts. Jack's arm is around his sister Eunice. Joe is in the center of the boat, and Rosemary and Kathleen are sitting together.

of Boston's well-to-do Irish Catholics summered at the livelier Nantasket; Cohasset was home to the old Boston families, and the Irish weren't welcome. That didn't stop Joe Kennedy from bringing his family there. But in 1922, when Mr. Kennedy tried to join the Cohasset Golf Club, the members who wanted no part of Joe Kennedy blackballed him. This rejection brought back painful memories of being excluded from Harvard's prestigious social clubs. Both were insults he would long remember.

While Mr. Kennedy fought the social wars, Jack had his own struggle—against ill health. The list of illnesses on his cards in Rose's file box grew longer and longer. By the time he was five years old, he had endured not only scarlet fever, but also whooping cough, measles, and chicken pox. The string of sicknesses began a pattern of poor health that would plague him throughout his life. Stomach problems, backaches, blurry vision, and mysterious symptoms that doctors couldn't diagnose such as fainting spells, weakness, and weight loss—beginning at a young age, Jack had them all.

It didn't seem fair. With so many children in his family, why was *he* the one who was so often stuck in bed? There was a silver lining to the dark cloud of all Jack's maladies, however. When he was sick, he often had his mother's undivided attention, a commodity that was in short supply.

Young Jack, so pale that his freckles stood out on his thin little face, would lie in bed and let his imagination flow along with Rose's voice as she read him stories. His great love of books, a passion that would last his lifetime, began in those early years as he listened to his mother read fairy tales and recite poetry.

Much later Mrs. Kennedy wrote that she worried Jack had not gotten the attention he needed as a child. It bothered her a great deal. Yet, despite Jack's perpetual illnesses, Mrs. Kennedy felt she had to devote her time and most of her concern to another child, her first daughter, Rosemary.

With two boys in the family, the Kennedys had been delighted when a girl was born to them in September 1918, fourteen months after Jack's birth. Mrs. Kennedy even gave the baby her own name, Rose, and added the middle name Marie. In the shorthand of the family, she became Rosemary. Rosemary was a pretty baby with green eyes that looked out placidly at the activity around her.

As an infant, Rosemary cried less than her brothers had, and she was slow to crawl and walk. With mounting concern, Mrs. Kennedy noted that she was slow to talk as well. Nor could Rosemary hold her spoon or help put on her clothes. Rose tried to tell herself that every child is different, that she shouldn't compare her daughter's rate of development with her sons'. But as Rosemary grew older, it became clear that something was wrong.

Her parents took her to doctor after doctor; her motor skills and intelligence were tested again and again. Finally there was a diagnosis: Rosemary was mentally retarded. But none of the health professionals could tell the Kennedys why this had happened or what, if anything, they could do about it. The best the doctors could suggest was that her parents put Rosemary in an institution.

In those days mental retardation was not only a condition to be dealt with, but also a cause of great shame. Families wanted to avoid the stigma of having a mentally challenged child in the house. At the same time, with almost nothing known about how to help these children, there was little hope for their future. So, on the advice of their doctors, parents often sent these children away—to facilities that ranged from tolerable to terrible. To Rose and Joe Kennedy's credit, they refused this option for Rosemary.

"What can they do for her in an institution that we can't do better for her here, at home with her family?" demanded Mr. Kennedy of the doctors. When the answer came back "nothing," Joe and Rose decided to keep Rosemary at home and raise her as normally as possible. She went to public school for kindergarten but had to repeat the year. Even then she was not allowed to pass into the first grade. So her parents hired tutors for

Rosemary. Though her abilities were never more than that of an eight- or nine-year-old, she learned to read, write, and do simple math. Her coordination remained weak, but growing up, she took the same swimming and dancing lessons her siblings did.

Like all the Kennedy children, Rosemary understood the value her family placed on winning. She, too, was imbued with a desire to succeed. For a child who was mentally challenged, however, this had both positive and negative aspects. There were always goals to strive for, whether it was learning to dance or to add and subtract. But there were deep frustrations for Rosemary, also, especially as it gradually became clear to her that she could never match the achievements of her brothers and sisters.

Outwardly, Rosemary looked much the same as the other children, and the Kennedys never told anyone about her condition. Jack and the others understood Rosemary's disability was information that was to be

From a young age, Jack learned to look out for his sister Rosemary.

kept strictly within the family. If anyone was bold enough to ask why Rosemary seemed somewhat different, they were told she was "quiet" or "shy."

Keeping a family secret must have been difficult and, at times, awkward. Jack never talked about how he felt having a sister who was mentally retarded, but like all the children in the family, he had to take responsibility for Rosemary's well-being. Joe and Jack were instructed to keep an eye on her when the children were out sledding or sailing or even taking a walk. Much later, when they were old enough to go to boy-girl parties, the brothers were told to dance with her and make sure their friends did the same. It was Eunice, one of Rosemary's younger sisters, who became her special friend and protector. As for Mrs. Kennedy, she worked with Rosemary tirelessly, teaching her to dress herself, to use proper table manners, and even to play tennis, bouncing a ball to her for hours on end.

Mrs. Kennedy's intentions were good, but all of the attention and effort she lavished on Rosemary was time taken away from the other children. Then, when Jack was five, Rose decided that she needed some time for herself. Her husband was often away on trips, for both business and pleasure. Now, she told him, she wanted to travel as well.

Mr. Kennedy was willing to indulge his wife, who had put aside her love of faraway places since her marriage. He agreed that he would try to be in town to oversee the household when Rose was away. The trips Rose looked forward to were not brief weekend jaunts. She wanted to travel across the country and to revisit Europe. All of this was quite unusual in the 1920s. Mothers didn't just go off for weeks at a time by themselves, and fathers were not usually very involved in raising the children.

But Joseph Kennedy was not your average father. Rose once called him "the architect of our lives." Determined to build a family that would be the centerpiece of his hopes and dreams, Mr. Kennedy was indeed a master designer with a grand plan. But to accomplish his goals, he had to make sure that he was the dominant influence in his children's lives. Joseph Kennedy ruled his family with a mixture of love, keen interest, and very high expectations.

Time with their father was something that all the children cherished. First of all, it was precious, since he was so frequently away. But when he was home, his attention was focused on them. When they were little, they would crawl into bed and cuddle with him while he read the newspaper comics aloud. As they became old enough to have conversations, he would encourage the children to talk to him about whatever they wanted. Rose said, "He would be responsive, understanding, amused or mock horrified, always affectionate, but if necessary corrective." When they were older, she remembered, "he treated them as equals, respecting each one as a unique and wonderfully interesting individual." Joe Kennedy had a way of really listening to his children and hearing their concerns. It made them feel secure in the knowledge that they were important and loved.

Eunice (left), Rosemary, Jack, Joe, and Kathleen in early 1920s, dressed for an outing. Mrs. Kennedy said that after school she let the boys dress like "roughnecks," but it was important to her that her children were well-groomed and tidy in public.

Yet even the pleasure of their father's attention didn't mean it was easy for the children to let their mother go away. Of all the young Kennedys, Jack was the one who gave vent to his emotions about her extended trips. At first, he used to cry when he saw her packing her bags. But after a while, he realized that this annoyed her terribly, so he quit.

"[It was] better to take it in stride," Jack recalled to a friend later, when he was a teenager.

At age five and a half, however, he hadn't yet learned to keep his thoughts to himself. Once, when Rose was leaving the next day for a six-week trip to California, Jack piped up, "Gee, you're a great mother to go away and leave your children alone."

Mrs. Kennedy was concerned about Jack's comment. After she'd said her good-byes, she returned to peek in the window to see how the children were doing. When she saw Jack playing with Joe, Rose decided that Jack had just been sassy when he made his remark—that he didn't really mind her leaving.

Perhaps Mrs. Kennedy truly believed this—or perhaps believing it eased her guilt. But she was mistaken. Jack did feel abandoned by his mother. It was bad enough to have to share her with his brother and three sisters. Now she was off having her own special adventures for weeks at a time.

Fortunately for Jack and the rest of the children, there was someone who filled in during their parents' absences—their grandfather Mayor John Fitzgerald. He was always eager to spend time with his grandchildren, showing them Boston, as years before he'd shown it to his favorite daughter, Rose. Small in stature, Mayor Fitzgerald was nonetheless larger than life. Known throughout Boston as "Honey Fitz" for his sweet way with words, he was famous for spouting poetry or bursting into his trademark song, "Sweet Adeline." A poem about him that appeared in a Boston paper began, "Honey Fitz can talk you blind / on any subject you can find." After a list of topics on which Mayor Fitzgerald could converse,

Rose (left) and her sister Agnes, wearing sombreros in Tijuana, Mexico. It was this West Coast trip that precipitated Jack's remark about Rose leaving her children to travel.

including motorboats, opening clams, and getting votes, the ditty ended, "On all these things and many more / Honey Fitz is crammed with lore." John Fitzgerald was a character, and both his family and his political supporters loved him for it.

Honey Fitz became a Democratic politician because almost all Irish voters in Boston were Democrats. It was the Democratic Party that had set up an infrastructure to assist the immigrant poor. In a time-honored trade-off, local political bosses would help the people in their neighborhoods with jobs, medical care, and food, in exchange for their votes. This system came to be known as machine politics (probably because the system ran like a well-oiled machine). It easily fell prey to corruption, but as mayor, Honey Fitz felt he was doing his best for the citizens of Boston.

As much as he enjoyed his two terms as mayor (1906–1907; 1910–1913), Honey Fitz truly loved his role as grandfather. He took the boys to baseball games at Fenway Park and gathered the children up to visit Boston Public Gardens and ride on the swan boats. Jack adored his grandfather. Whenever he would hear his car drive up to the house, Jack would rush to the door yelling, "It's Grandpa!"

If Honey Fitz's presence in Jack's life cheered him up during his parents' absences, there was one change in routine when they went away that annoyed him considerably. Although the nanny and other hired help were ultimately responsible for their charges' welfare, Mr. and Mrs. Kennedy left instructions that the children were also supposed to pay attention to Joe Jr.

Joe accepted this responsibility seriously and somewhat gleefully. "I'm in charge," he'd crow to Jack. As he grew older, Joe Jr. often took it upon himself to issue orders to the servants about what sort of discipline should be meted out to his siblings. He would also advise them what his parents would do in any given situation. On Sundays, if his parents were gone, Joe Jr. would sit at the head of the table and carve the roast. Mr. and Mrs. Kennedy, who thought Joe could do very little wrong, were

As mayor of Boston, John "Honey Fitz" Fitzgerald (right) met with many dignitaries. Here, he shakes hands with President William Howard Taft in 1912.

delighted to know that their eldest son was helping to keep things running in their absence.

For Jack, having no parents around meant more times when he was expected to knuckle under to his brother. Joe's position of power was one more piece of evidence that no matter how hard Jack tried, he could never occupy Joe's place in the family—or in his parents' hearts.

What Jack probably did not understand was that being the favored child must have been wearying at times. Joe Jr. was expected to do the right thing, to be dependable, to act, sometimes, like a small adult. Friends remembered him sneaking away occasionally to relax in the relative quiet of their homes. But his sense of responsibility never deserted him. He once informed a pal with the utmost seriousness, "You know, I'm the oldest of my family, and I've got to be the example."

It's likely that Jack occasionally dreamed about being the eldest Kennedy brother. In reality, that role was more difficult to play than he imagined.

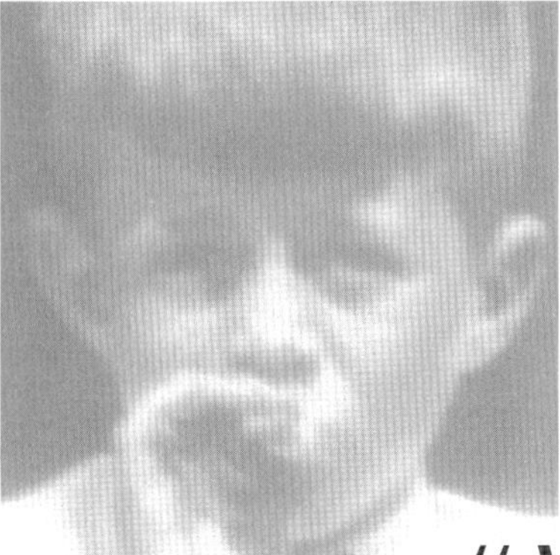

"WEAVING DAYDREAMS"

CHAPTER IV

The first school that Jack Kennedy attended had an odd name—Devotion. The name had nothing to do with religion; Devotion was the nearby public school. It was named for Edward Devotion, a Brookline town constable in the seventeenth century. With its old-fashioned gabled roof, the school was a familiar sight to the Kennedy brothers from their jaunts around the neighborhood.

In 1921, six-year-old Joe walked the few blocks to Devotion wearing a tie and short pants, as was the custom. At first, he didn't like school. He was especially poor in art. With the help of a nice student teacher, however, he gained more confidence. Soon he had settled down and was working to be the best in his class. Jack started school at Devotion the following year. Yet before he could get settled in, he was forced to stay home for several weeks with the flu.

From a very early age, Jack Kennedy had a keen wit and a way with words. He took delight in amusing people, disarming them with his clever "take" on what was going on around him. His mother said, "He was a funny little boy, and he said things in such an original vivid way."

Jack with Rosemary and their grandfather P.J. Kennedy. Jack is pretending to smoke a cigar, but his grandfather probably did not appreciate the joke. As an adult, Jack recalled the family's weekly visits to the home of his Kennedy grandparents: "On those Sunday visits, my grandfather would not let us cut up or even wink in his presence."

Mrs. Kennedy didn't find everything funny. Once, she proudly told her children about the time she and her younger sister Agnes went to the White House to visit President McKinley. "President McKinley said my seven-year-old sister was the prettiest girl who had ever visited the White House," Mrs. Kennedy informed her brood.

"But Mother," queried Jack, "why didn't he say it about you?"

Still, Mrs. Kennedy was taken enough by Jack's novel way of expressing himself that the year Jack was six, she wrote down some of the things he said in her journal.

When his first-grade teacher was about to arrive for a home visit, and Jack suspected she planned to discuss his daydreaming in class, he informed his parents, "You know, I am getting on all right, and if you study too much, you're liable to go crazy!"

Another time he remarked, "Daddy has a sweet tooth. I wonder which one it is?"

At Easter, when the family was on their way to St. Aiden's for the Good Friday service, Mrs. Kennedy told her children that they should wish for a happy death. Jack said he preferred to wish for two dogs.

As much as Rose was amused by Jack's unique way of putting together his thoughts, of seeing and doing things his own way, those same qualities could also annoy her. As Rose herself later said, "Now and then, fairly often in fact, that distressed me, since I thought I knew what was best."

Jack and his mother were also at loggerheads over her many rules. In a large family, it's hard to get things accomplished if everyone is off doing his or her own thing. So Mrs. Kennedy did whatever she could think of to organize her children, right down to lining them up in the bathroom by order of age to brush their teeth.

Two values that Mrs. Kennedy stressed were tidiness and punctuality, especially for meals. The household ran more smoothly when the children paid attention to picking up their things and being prompt. Jack, dreamy and perhaps a little defiant, was neither neat nor on time.

Young Joe made sure he was never late for meals. Bobby, the Kennedy's seventh child, was once so worried about being late for dinner that he ran through the house and crashed through a glass door.

But Jack, who lived by his own clock, often came wandering into the dining room after everyone was seated. The rule was, if you missed the first or even the second course, you could eat only what was being served at the moment. Sometimes Jack was so tardy, he had to settle for just a couple of spoonfuls of dessert.

Later he would sneak into the kitchen and charm Kico or one of the other servants into giving him some food. Mrs. Kennedy knew this was happening and was torn. On one hand, it offended her sense of discipline that Jack should be given food when he had disobeyed the rules. On the other, since he was such a sickly, skinny child, he needed the nutrition. Sometimes she pretended she didn't know that he was getting the left-overs.

There was another reason Mr. and Mrs. Kennedy insisted on punctuality when it came to meals. The dining room was a place for more than just eating. Wanting their children to feel confident about their ideas and to be articulate in discussing them, Rose and Joe decided that the young Kennedys should first learn how to speak up at the dinner table.

Rose and Joe didn't want just idle conversation, however. So, near the dining room, Mrs. Kennedy put up a bulletin board where she would post newspaper articles and other bits of historical or religious information. As the children got old enough to read, they were supposed to scan the bulletin board and have something to say at dinnertime about the posted topics.

Looking back, Mrs. Kennedy remembered how she led some of the discussions: "A Florida item could cue me to ask how the state got its name. What did the word mean, what language is it from? Think of Spanish names of towns. . . . Where else in the country are there lots of Spanish names? Yes, California. What about San Francisco, what does that mean? Who was it named after?"

The conversations at the family dinner table were yet another place where Jack and Joe, both full of opinions, competed for attention. One habit, however, was Jack's alone, and it made his parents, especially his mother, very happy. Jack was a reader, tearing through books as fast as he could turn the pages.

Jack had a desire to read that Joe Jr. never acquired. Ironically, the illnesses that punctuated his young life gave him extra time to do what he loved. Flat on his back, removed from his rough-and-tumble family, Jack lived through his reading. Books cushioned him from the pain and discomfort of his poor health.

When he first began reading, Jack followed the escapades of Reddy Fox by Thornton Burgess. Decades later, after he became president of the

Rose Kennedy and her first five children—Eunice (on lap), Kathleen, Rosemary (sitting), Jack (on tricycle), and Joe Jr.—circa 1922. Eunice was especially close to Rosemary. As an adult, Eunice spearheaded the Special Olympics for children with mental disabilities.

United States, he was delighted to receive from Mr. Burgess an autographed copy of *The Adventures of Reddy Fox*.

Jack's affection for Reddy Fox was surpassed only by his love of a goat named Billy Whiskers. The independent goat did whatever he felt like doing—one reason, perhaps, why he appealed to Jack. If someone bothered Billy, he butted him out of the way. Billy Whiskers and his family traveled the world, having adventures, and Jack devoured the whole series of books about them.

As much as Mrs. Kennedy approved of Jack's reading habits, she did not care for Billy Whiskers. In her opinion, the books were garishly illustrated, and the stories were a waste of time. If her mother, Grandma Fitzgerald, hadn't given the books to Jack, Rose declared, she wouldn't have let them in the house.

One day, Jack came to his mother and asked, "Where are the Sandwich Islands?"

Mrs. Kennedy didn't know, but she said she'd find out. Later she opened an atlas and showed them to Jack. They were located in the Pacific Ocean and now were called the Hawaiian Islands.

"Why are you interested in the islands?" Mrs. Kennedy asked him. "Are you studying them in school?"

"No," Jack responded, "but Billy Whiskers has stopped at the Sandwich Islands on his way across the Pacific Ocean."

Mrs. Kennedy had to admit that even books she thought unsuitable might spark a child's imagination.

As Jack grew older, his health always up and down, he spent many, many hours reading. He especially loved books that could take him other places, far from his sickbed. He fought with the pirates in *Treasure Island* and lived with the animals in *Bambi* and *Black Beauty*. He was inspired and excited by the chivalry and heroic adventures of King Arthur and his Knights of the Round Table, stories he read again and again.

Reading developed gifts in Jack that Joe didn't share to nearly the same

Jack—First Communion. Jack is dressed up for this important milestone in his life as a young Catholic.

degree: imagination and the ability to be intensely caught up in a private, unseen world. Reading also taught Jack how to think about and understand events outside his own experience. Despite Joe's superiority in health and strength, to say nothing of his hold on his parents' affection, Joe envied the way reading allowed Jack to set himself apart, to be "the intellectual" of the family, as his sister Eunice once called him.

When Jack was feeling fine, however, he seemed to have a unique ability to make mischief. Once, Kico heard him calling to some of his friends in the street, but she couldn't find him. Then the nanny saw Jack and was horrified—he had climbed out the bathroom window and onto the roof. Together Kico and Mrs. Kennedy tried to coax him inside, bribing him with candy and toys, but he was having too much fun. At last, when he was good and ready, he crawled in. His mother was relieved and angry—it was a thirty-foot drop from the roof to the ground.

Another time, Jack hid out in the cellar after teasing a little girl so unmercifully that she complained to a passing policeman. Jack, just returned from a sleepover, said, "Well, here I have been home only a few hours and the cops are chasing me already!"

Jack's shenanigans led to punishment, and he sometimes found himself on the wrong end of the ruler or wooden hanger Mrs. Kennedy used to spank her children. Physical punishment was not Mr. Kennedy's style. When he was angry, he would turn an intimidating glare at whoever was misbehaving and tell the child to stop "the monkeyshines" or "cut out the applesauce."

Rose, however, was influenced by several books on child rearing that encouraged mothers to be spare in giving affection and strict about discipline. She didn't dole out many hugs or cuddles, but she did deliver a fair number of whacks on the behind. They were never given in anger. Mrs. Kennedy simply felt young children needed punishment that was "swift and sure." Wily Jack, copying two naughty comic-strip characters, the Katzenjammer Kids, sometimes stuffed a pillow down his pants to soften

Jack with one of the several dogs the Kennedy family owned while the children were growing up. Jack was also fond of horses and enjoyed riding. When Jack was seven, visiting Maine, he wrote to Rose, ". . . we go out avry [every] day and the horse are good. and one of the horse are lazy and [h]is name is Happy he can run if he wants to. but hees a good horse just the same."

the blows. That made his mother smile—and occasionally she let him get away with it.

What bothered Rose Kennedy most about her second son—more than any of his misbehavior—was his lack of attention to the details of life that were so important to her. Almost everything Jack did ran counter to Mrs. Kennedy's love of order and organization. Here was a boy who was amusing and clever, but who couldn't obey the family's most basic rules. This disobedience was a trial to her and a source of puzzlement, yet her feelings were also tinged with a grudging admiration. Looking back Rose Kennedy remembered, "He had a strong romantic and idealistic streak. In fact, he was inclined to be somewhat of a dreamer. I often had the feeling his mind was only half-occupied with the subject at hand, such as doing his arithmetic homework or picking up his clothes off the floor. The rest of his thoughts were far away, weaving daydreams."

"A REAL STIGMA"

CHAPTER V

If young Jack was a weaver of daydreams, his father was man of big ideas—with the dynamic energy to turn them into reality. Again and again, he had demonstrated this ability—by getting into Harvard, where he helped finance his schooling by owning and operating a Boston tour bus, and in his varied and successful business dealings. As a businessman, Joseph Kennedy was unique because he seemed to have a second sense about which kinds of businesses would be successful and which would fail. He didn't want to make money just to be rich; he wanted to use his fortune as a basis to advance his family, socially and politically. In 1924, Mr. Kennedy was ready to put his big ideas for his children's future into motion.

Rose Kennedy wanted her children to attend Catholic school or to stay in public schools like Devotion, "where they'd meet the grocer's son and the plumber's son . . . They could have seen that some of those boys were even brighter than they were." Joe Kennedy had something quite different in mind. He knew that the kind of success he wanted for his children would come only if they could "make it" outside of Irish-Catholic society. "Making it" began with sending his boys to the best schools, where they could compete with—and beat—the sons of the very people who were so intent on excluding the Irish.

Although he cared deeply about his daughters and was interested in their futures, it was his sons in whom Mr. Kennedy was really invested. His hopes and dreams were pinned on them. He conceded the responsibility for his daughters' education to his wife. The girls could go to Catholic school, if that was what Rose preferred. His boys would attend elite private schools.

So, in the fall of 1924, when Jack was seven and Joe nine, the boys transferred from Devotion to an all-male school in Brookline, where the students were the sons of the wealthy and privileged. Dexter (originally called Nobles and Greenough) charged tuition of $400 a year. It offered a

The Dexter football team. Joe Jr. is sitting third from the left in the second row. Jack is sitting cross-legged in the lower right-hand corner.

Joe Jr. and Jack (around seven years old) in a friendly pose, though neither boy looks particularly happy

full school day, from 8:15 to 4:45, but the last couple of hours were devoted to organized sports, an important part of the school's curriculum.

On their first day, Joe and Jack headed off to Dexter attired in the school uniform of short pants, long stockings, and a red sweater. Mrs. Kennedy, to her sons' embarrassment, had knitted a hood on each boy's sweater to ward off the cold. But the Kennedy brothers had more to contend with than simple embarrassment about the right clothing. Almost everyone at Dexter was Protestant, and snobbery ran rampant. "We were probably the only Irish Catholics there," Jack remembered as an adult. The other students were well aware of the distinction.

One of Jack's classmates later recalled that the boys who went to Dexter were prejudiced against the Irish. They freely repeated things they heard their families say—that the Irish were dishonest or dirty, for example. "To be Irish Catholic was a real, real stigma," the classmate remembered. When the other boys got mad at the Kennedys, they would resort to calling them "Irish" or "Catholic," using the words as ethnic slurs.

Joe and Jack reacted to that sort of taunting differently, and each boy's behavior was typical of his personality. A hotheaded Joe would challenge the name-callers to a fight. Jack would coolly bet with the other boys on his brother's ability to win the battle. The wager was for a coveted collectible—marbles—and Jack usually came home with a bag of them.

The Dexter students probably also heard their parents' whispers about Mr. Kennedy's unsavory business practices. During the era of Prohibition, 1919 to 1933, when alcohol was outlawed in the United States, it was rumored that Joe Kennedy worked with bootleggers, who smuggled liquor into the country. People suspected Mr. Kennedy made sizable profits off of the illegal activity. As a stockbroker, it was said he used "insider trading," driving stock prices up and down to his own advantage, a dubious if not illegal practice. Many of the Dexter students' parents would have nothing to do with Joseph Kennedy.

It also did not help the Kennedy brothers that their grandfather, Honey

Fitz, was stereotyped by many as the quintessential Irish politician—loud, overbearing, willing to trade favors for votes. To the old Bostonians, the former mayor was representative of those who had wrested political power away from them. (In fact, in his mayoral bid of 1910, Honey Fitz had defeated the grandfather of one of the Kennedy brothers' Dexter classmates, James Jackson Storrow III.) Any knock against Honey Fitz must have particularly bothered Jack, who took an early interest in politics because of his grandfather. Jack had even "campaigned" with Honey Fitz when he was running (unsuccessfully, as it turned out) for the governorship of Massachusetts in 1923. The old man had used six-year-old Jack as a sounding board in that race, plunking him down and trying out his speeches on the boy. During that campaign, Jack made his first public appearance.

After speaking to a group of supporters, Honey Fitz lifted Jack onto a table and proclaimed, "Here's my grandson, the finest grandson in the world!" To which Jack replied, "My grandpa is the finest grandpa in the world!" The crowd cheered Jack's "speech."

Despite the prejudice they experienced at Dexter, both boys flourished there. Except for a male sports coach, the staff was made up of devoted women teachers. Led by a stalwart principal, Miss Myra Fiske, these teachers were dedicated to their students' education, invoking the school motto, "Today our best, tomorrow better." The classes were small, and the boys were drilled continuously in math and grammar. Memory work and speaking in front of others were also important parts of the learning process. The boys had to recite in unison notable pieces of writing, like Lincoln's Gettysburg Address.

Jack was a favorite of Miss Fiske's. She especially appreciated his growing interest in history. The stirrings of this interest, which became a passion as he grew older, probably came from his mother. Rose Kennedy got her own love of history from Honey Fitz. He had dreamed of becoming a doctor, but after his parents died, he took on the responsibility of caring for his eight brothers. To earn money, he led walking tours through

Boston's historic North End, referring to "these narrow streets where history seems to come alive." The more he learned about Boston, the more Honey Fitz came to love it. When he was a father, he made sure Rose and his other children were intimately acquainted with this cradle of American democracy.

Mrs. Kennedy was equally intent on having her own children learn about U.S. history. Massachusetts, one of the thirteen original colonies, was certainly a good place to start. She took her children to see sites like Plymouth Rock, where the Pilgrims landed, and to Bunker and Breed's Hills where, in the summer of 1775, raw, untrained colonial farmers first proved they could stand up to the British redcoats.

In Boston, there were just as many things to see: Faneuil Hall, the marketplace where Yankee Patriots made inspiring speeches claiming "no taxation without representation"; Old South Meeting House, where angry colonists, objecting to the tax on tea, planned the Boston Tea Party; and Old North Church, in whose steeple were displayed the two lanterns that signaled British troop movements to Paul Revere.

Jack, whose imagination was already ignited with the derring-do of the princes and pirates he'd met in fairy tales, was just as enamored of American heroes like George Washington and Paul Revere.

Once, Jack told Miss Fiske that if she would take him to the Revolutionary War battle sites of Lexington and Concord, Mr. Kennedy would provide his Rolls-Royce for the trip. On the day of the excursion, many of the students turned out to get a look at one of the fanciest and most expensive cars on the road. But when the Kennedy car pulled up, it was only an old Model T Ford, much to the humiliation of Jack, who had to endure the jokes and jeers of his classmates. The Rolls-Royce was apparently being used elsewhere.

Sports were a major focus at Dexter. The school had four acres of playing fields. Young athletes could take their pick: football, baseball, tennis, even ice hockey. Joe Jr. and Jack were anxious to join the football team, and Mr. Kennedy was eager for the boys to show their "stuff" as well. In sports, the brothers could virtually level the playing field between themselves and those boys who thought they were better than the Kennedys. Despite his frequent absences from home, in the fall of 1926, Mr. Kennedy made sure he was in Brookline to take Joe Jr. and Jack to their first football practice.

Joe, stocky and sturdy, was built for football. He showed off his aggressiveness by running through the defensive line rather than trying to evade it. But Jack, quick and fast, had a nimble athletic ability beyond Joe's. To Jack's delight, for once he was able to pull ahead of Joe; that his success was in the competitive field of sports made his achievements all the sweeter. He was the quarterback of the Dexter team, and he must have been thrilled to be named its captain. Jack was also named captain of the baseball team. To his delight, on the day of a big game there was a telegram from his father addressed to *Captain Jack Kennedy.* As Jack grew up, however, one of his lingering illnesses became a bad back. After Dexter, he would never again top his brother on the playing field.

The boys settled in at Dexter. They eventually made friends and were getting decent grades. So it came as a shock when it was announced that the school was going to close and the land sold to a developer. Mr. Kennedy, impressed with the quality of education at Dexter, took it upon himself to organize a group of parents who bought the school. Miss Fiske was kept on as principal, and Mr. Kennedy put himself on the school board. The other parents may have gossiped about the business practices that helped make Mr. Kennedy rich, but they didn't seem to mind when he used his money and influence to keep the school open.

Considering all the effort that had gone into the purchase and reorganization of Dexter, it seemed as though the Kennedy brothers were going to be at the school for the long haul. The boys were just getting ready for the fall term in 1927—Joe was going into sixth grade; Jack, age ten, into fifth—when Mr. Kennedy decided to make a drastic change in his family's life.

Jack Kennedy, captain and quarterback of the Dexter football team

More and more, his business endeavors were taking him out of Boston. In 1924, he had spent so much time working on a business deal in New York City that he didn't see his sixth child, daughter Patricia, until she was a month old. When he finally arrived in Boston, his family came to greet him at the railroad station.

"Daddy, Daddy, we have another baby," Joe, Jack, Rosemary, Kathleen, and Eunice yelled. Mr. Kennedy noticed the other travelers staring at him. "I'm sure they were thinking the last thing that fellow needs is another baby!"

In the mid-1920s, with a fortune of about $2 million at his disposal, Joseph Kennedy had decided to get into an exciting new field, the movie business. Having started from simple twelve-minute chase scenes called "one-reelers," the movies, though silent, now featured dramatic plots with elaborate backdrops. The business was still in its infancy, but Mr. Kennedy could see only growth ahead—and a fortune to be made. He called films "a gold mine." In 1922, he purchased his first movie theater. Then, in 1925, he bought a movie studio called FBO (Film Bookings Office), which produced mostly cowboy films and action-filled adventures. Now Mr. Kennedy had to travel back and forth to California, the hub of the movie industry. It was easier to take trains (the most common form of long-distance transportation back then) from New York City to Los Angeles than it was to depart from Boston. So Mr. Kennedy made the decision to pull up stakes and move his family to New York.

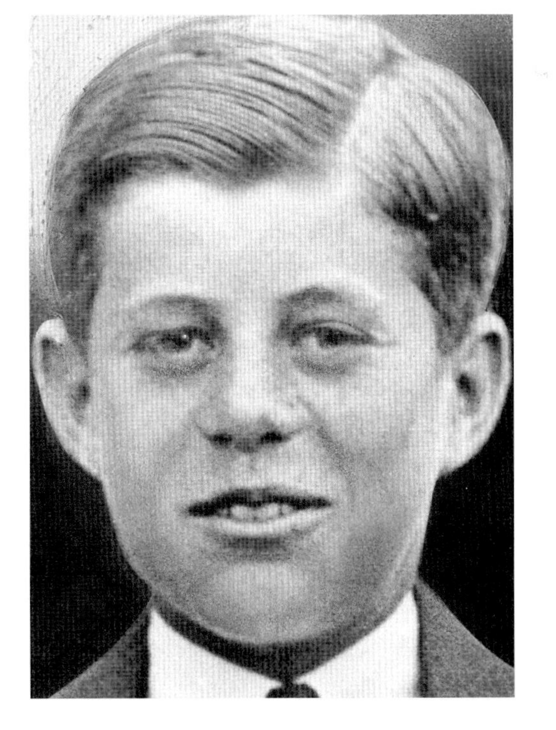

Jack at ten, around the time the Kennedys moved to New York

There was also another, more personal reason for Joe Kennedy's decision to move his family out of Boston. He was sick and tired of the social prejudice that seemed to dog him at every turn. Two years before the move, he had been turned down for membership at the exclusive Brookline Country Club. It was a cruel reminder of his rejections by the prestigious clubs at Harvard and by the Cohasset Golf Club. Years later, Joe Kennedy said he left Boston because it was no place to raise Irish-Catholic children. "I didn't want them to go through what I had to go through when I was growing up there."

So, in the fall of 1927, the Kennedy family packed up their belongings and their memories from the storybook house on Naples and Abbottsford Roads and prepared to move from Brookline to a rented thirteen-room mansion in Riverdale, New York, just north of Manhattan, the heart of bustling New York City. They would live there until a suitable estate could be found to purchase.

Leaving everything and everyone you know isn't easy, no matter what your age. The older children—Joe, Jack, Rosemary, Kathleen, and Eunice—would have to adjust to new schools and make new friends. Things would be a little easier for three-year-old Patricia and Bobby, almost two, who had been born in 1925. But all of the children would miss their relatives, especially Honey Fitz. Mrs. Kennedy, now pregnant with her eighth child, also had mixed emotions about moving away from her lifelong home. She had tried to put it off as long as possible.

Sympathetic to his family's feelings, Mr. Kennedy decided that he would make the actual move an event to remember. He rented a private railroad car, just for the family and the servants, in which to make the trip. On September 26, 1927, their train pulled out of the South Street station, with the family ensconced in its well-appointed accommodations, dining on a catered lunch. The Fitzgeralds and the Kennedys may have come to Boston in filthy coffin ships, but the current crop of Kennedys was moving out in style.

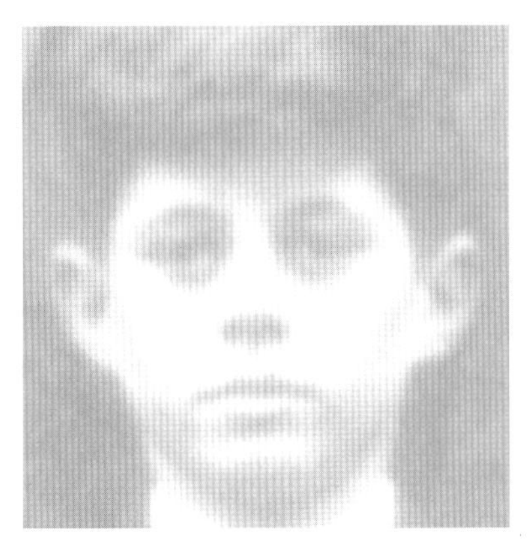

HYANNIS PORT AND HOLLYWOOD

CHAPTER VI

The Kennedys' new home, in exclusive Riverdale, New York, sat on a bluff overlooking the Hudson River. The community was just twelve miles north of Manhattan, but the environment was rural. Jack, Joe, and Kathleen—but not Rosemary or the little children—were allowed to play in the woods behind the house, a perfect place for hide-and-seek. As Jack roamed the grounds, he could see sheep grazing on the grass of nearby estates or watch the Hudson River flowing toward the Atlantic Ocean—an inviting landscape for a boy who liked to dream.

Even though the Riverdale house was larger and more palatial than their home in Brookline, and despite the new things to do and places to visit—like fast-paced, glittering New York City where their father had offices—it was hard for Jack to start over. Despite Mr. Kennedy's statements about leaving Boston because of prejudice, he had nevertheless put his family in another environment that was not particularly welcoming.

One reason the Kennedys selected Riverdale as their new home was its proximity to the well-respected Riverdale Country School, which the

older boys would be attending. Victorian buildings and an expanse of playing fields added to the school's appeal. Yet once again, the students were mostly Protestant, with few Catholics in attendance.

Nor were there many Catholics in Riverdale. Although the area had several Presbyterian and Episcopalian churches, the closest Catholic church was about five miles away in the city of Yonkers. Since most of the people who lived in Riverdale were Republicans, the Democratic Kennedys were doubly outsiders. A classmate of Jack's at Riverdale remembered that the Kennedys "were like fish out of water because of their lifestyle, their close-knit family, their father's lack of participation in neighborhood activities, and their mother's Catholic activities, which few if any of the neighborhood families shared."

Rose Kennedy was so unhappy in Riverdale that she went back to Boston to deliver her eighth child, Jean, in February of 1928. But it was not just the new locale that was bothering Mrs. Kennedy. Her relationship

Jack and his classmates at Riverdale Country School, circa 1928. Jack is in the center of the first row.

with her husband was also changing. Joseph Kennedy had always had an eye for the ladies. Now, through his involvement with films, he had met the beautiful movie star Gloria Swanson and begun a romantic relationship with her.

Rose and Joe Kennedy had started out as a love match. They began dating as teenagers, and the couple soon considered themselves "sweethearts." Honey Fitz was not as enamored. First he said that they were too young to be involved. Then he came up with another beau for Rose—one whom he liked better. He certainly didn't mind that Rose's European schooling also kept the young lovers apart. What could have been wrong with ambitious Joe Kennedy? Honey Fitz may not have wanted Rose dating the son of his sometime political rival, P.J. Kennedy. Or perhaps he recognized that the formidable Joe might interfere with the strong relationship he shared with his daughter. Rose tried to abide by Honey Fitz's wishes, but she couldn't resist Joe. The young couple often met secretly until Joe graduated from Harvard and began his successful career in banking. By then, Honey Fitz could come up with no further objections, and Rose and Joe were married in 1914.

The euphoria Rose felt at finally surmounting all the obstacles and settling down with Joe flagged under the weight of home and children—and her husband's infidelities. Rose turned a blind eye to the other women, but the knowledge of them took a toll on her marriage. Divorce was not common in those days, and in any case, the Catholic church did not permit it. Rose was too devout to consider dissolving her marriage. As the years went on, Rose and Joe's relationship became less a conventional marriage and more a business partnership—and the business was building successful young Kennedys.

How much Jack knew about his parents' relationship while he was growing up is a question. His parents didn't fight; they were always polite to each other; and they usually agreed about how to raise their children. Each certainly admired things about the other. Rose thought Joe was an excellent father and, of course, provider; Joe appreciated Rose's intelli-

Rose Fitzgerald and Joseph Kennedy were married in October 1914, in a small service attended only by their families and close friends. But as the daughter of the former mayor, the wedding merited this photograph in The Boston Globe.

gence and often praised her ability as the family organizer. What Jack would have noticed was that his father's absences were more frequent and longer once he became involved with running a movie studio, and that his mother seemed very lonely in Riverdale.

Although he was never close to his mother, as an adult Jack remembered that Rose "was the glue that kept the family together." This was never more true than during Joe Kennedy's Hollywood years, which began in 1925 and ended in 1930, when Mr. Kennedy sold most of his movie holdings. Around the same time, he ended his affair with Gloria Swanson. After returning permanently to New York and resuming his business dealings, Joe and Rose seemed happier than they had been in many years. Joe, no doubt, was pleased with the way Rose had managed the family "enterprise" on her own for months at a time. Rose must have breathed a sigh of relief that Gloria Swanson was no longer in their lives. The lesson for the children was that whatever their differences, their parents were still committed to their relationship and to their family.

Mr. and Mrs. Kennedy were leading by example. They always insisted that despite internal squabbles and jealousies, the Kennedy children should stand up for one another and present a united front to the outside world. In Riverdale, away from everything that was familiar, Jack and his siblings did band together, molding themselves into the Kennedy "clan," as Joe Jr. dubbed them. One childhood friend recalled, "No matter what anyone else had done, the Kennedy children always praised each other's accomplishments to the skies."

By the spring of 1928, in the midst of Mr. Kennedy's Hollywood years, as New York was becoming home, the eight young Kennedys ranged in age from twelve-year-old Joe to baby Jean. They were all attractive, sharing the family looks of reddish-brown hair, light-colored eyes in shades from blue to gray to green, and faces sprinkled with freckles. Their natural exuberance was tempered with a will to win and the stern injunction against crybabies. Another of Mr. Kennedy's oft-repeated dictums, along with "we want winners," was "we don't want any crying in this house."

Around the time he moved his family to New York, Joe Kennedy also bought the home they had been renting for several years in Hyannis Port, on Cape Cod. The rambling white house with green shutters and a front lawn that sloped to the edge of the sea was set on two acres. The grounds were large enough to accommodate a private tennis court and a swimming pool.

As with many of the things he did, Mr. Kennedy had a hidden reason for his decision to purchase the Hyannis Port house. Though he rarely mentioned his political ambitions, Joseph Kennedy harbored a secret wish to be president of the United States. Wealthy, powerful, and an important contributor to the Democratic Party, Mr. Kennedy felt he had all the qualifications to be president. He was also smart enough to realize that in 1928, the country was still too prejudiced against Catholics to elect one as president.

The sprawling white house in Hyannis Port, Massachusetts, where the Kennedys spent their summers. It is still used by family members today.

In a country that was overwhelmingly Protestant, Catholics were viewed with suspicion. Their church rites seemed strange to many. Some people suspected that they were more loyal to the pope, the head of the Catholic Church, than they were to the United States. Many Catholics were recent immigrants. Their ways and sometimes their languages (as with Italian or Polish Catholics, for instance) were different from the majority, and so the newcomers were often looked down upon and denied opportunities. This often remains true even today for minority religions and races in America.

Despite these prejudiced attitudes, Joe Kennedy felt there was a good chance things would change by the time his namesake, Joe Jr., was old enough to run for office. All of Mr. Kennedy's hopes for his children began coalescing into a great dream for his eldest son—that one day Joe Jr. would become the first Catholic president of the United States.

After all, on the day Joe Jr. had been born, Honey Fitz told a reporter, "Is he going into politics? Well, of course, he's going to be President of the United States; his mother and father have already decided that he is going to Harvard, where he will play on the football and baseball teams and incidentally take all the honors. Then he is going to be a captain of industry until it's time for him to be President."

Honey Fitz appeared to be speaking tongue in cheek about his newborn grandchild. But perhaps he was casting his shrewd politician's eye toward the future. Many of his predictions for Joe Jr. turned out to be true. In any case, with young Joe's possible political career in mind, Mr. Kennedy decided to keep one foot in Massachusetts, where his father's and his father-in-law's well-established connections to the Democratic Party might one day be very important to his firstborn.

The sprawling house in Hyannis Port was not as palatial as some the Kennedys would later occupy, but it was large and comfortable and became the hub of the family, especially after the children grew older and went away to boarding school. In some ways the Kennedy children were like two separate families. Joe Jr., Jack, and Kathleen formed one group. Eunice bridged the gap to the younger ones, Patricia, Bobby, Jean, and Teddy, who would join the family in 1932 when Joe Jr. was almost seventeen years old. Rosemary was close to Eunice, but her playmates were her younger siblings, who mentally outgrew her, one by one. Given this wide age range among the children, and their parents' constant travel, it was sometimes hard for the family to connect. At Hyannis Port, parents and children could gather each summer to swim, sail, walk along the beach, play games, and just be together.

For Jack, vacations at the shore had represented some of the happiest times of his life. Once the family was ensconced in Hyannis Port, the connection became permanent. Jack loved the ocean and felt as natural swimming or boating as he did strolling along the sand dunes, breathing in the salty air. Being close to the water made the boy who was sick so often feel especially alive, and this feeling remained true and strong throughout his life.

Both Joe Jr. and Jack had learned to sail at an early age. Their father was happy to provide them sailboats and lessons, even though he knew nothing about sailing himself. When they first began taking boats out, the boys were so small that, from a distance, it seemed the vessels were empty. By the time the Kennedys moved to Hyannis Port, Joe and Jack were accomplished sailors. After one sailing race, when Joe was twelve and Jack ten, they were relaxing on the porch of their house when they noticed a man clinging to the side of his disabled boat. Rushing to their sailboat, the *Rose Elizabeth*, they sped out and saved the man. Mr. Kennedy made sure the rescue was written up in the newspaper, which reported it as "daring."

Jack was about twelve when he was given his own craft, which he named *Victura*. He wasn't sure exactly what the word meant, but he knew it had something to do with victory, and that seemed appropriate for the Kennedy household. Mr. and Mrs. Kennedy found summer, with its sailing races, tennis matches, and swim meets, an excellent time to reiterate how much winning mattered. Coming in first was important, sister Eunice remembered. "Coming in second was just no good."

As usual, Joe Jr. took his parents' words to heart. The way he figured it, if you were going to make an effort, you might as well win. Jack was less certain. Winning was great, but doing things his way offered its own satisfactions—a concept his parents didn't seem to understand. Besides, some of the things he most liked to do, such as reading, didn't lend themselves to the easy formula of winning and losing.

Nevertheless, like all his siblings, Jack found himself participating in various summer competitions and contests. In the larger, neighboring town of Hyannis, their parents entered the children in all the swimming and boating races. And, as their father wanted, they usually won.

In between competitions, there were other planned activities at the Hyannis Port home. The young Kennedys were expected out on the lawn by 7 A.M. for calisthenics, led by one of the physical-education teachers their father hired as summer tutors for his children. Then the day might bring golf, swimming, and sailing lessons. Tennis was taught on the Kennedys' private court. Naturally, with this much activity, the Hyannis Port house was a busy, noisy place. All day long it rang with banging doors, laughing, screaming, the sounds of having fun.

The neighbors, many of whom were unhappy that the Kennedy kids were snapping up the local prizes, disliked the constant noise. Jack and his siblings didn't care much what the neighbors thought. They went on with their activities, including ferocious touch-football games that they continued to enjoy even after they became adults. The girls participated in these as eagerly as the boys. Kathleen, especially, loved the fierce encounters, going out for passes and agilely catching the balls her brothers threw to her. One acquaintance noted: "They are the most competitive and at the same time the most cohesive family I've ever seen. They fight each other, yet they feed on each other. They stimulate each other. Their minds strike sparks."

In the case of Jack and Joe, their fists also struck a few sparks. Joe and Jack often brought the rough-and-tumble physicality of the football games inside, and by the time they moved to Hyannis Port, the brothers' wranglings were legendary in the family. Young Bobby was so terrified by Jack and Joe's fistfights that when they started in on each other, he would run upstairs in tears, cover his ears, and hide. Once, he even heard Joe banging Jack's head against their bedroom wall.

Although the fighting always seemed to start over some petty upset of the day, it was really about which brother would come out on top. In some ways, it was amazing that Jack was still engaged in the battle. Joe

Joe Jr. and Jack in their identical swimsuits. Sisters Rosemary, Kathleen, Eunice, and Patricia (from right to left) are also dressed alike, because Mrs. Kennedy felt it was easier to identify her children in the water that way. Only young Bobby and baby Jean didn't have anyone to be matched with.

had clearly won the title of the most important child in the family. Jack must have known he was never going to be number one in his parents' hearts. Nevertheless, he was going to go down swinging—literally. It probably annoyed Joe terribly that Jack refused to learn his place and concede Joe his.

One of Joe and Jack's more dangerous encounters occurred at the beach. The boys had matching bathing suits, and Jack put on Joe's by mistake. Typically, Joe erupted. Rose stepped in and assured Joe that it would never happen again. A few days later, however, Jack—accidentally, or maybe not—once more slipped on the wrong suit. This time their mother wasn't around. In a fury, Joe took off after Jack, who started running—across the lawn, through the marsh, and down to the churning ocean. Jack sprinted alongside the crumbling old breakwall, with Joe gaining on him every step of the way. Fortunately, a family friend saw them and rushed over, ordering Joe and Jack out of the water as they started pummeling each other with the waves crashing dangerously around them.

The noisy Hyannis Port house did hold one attraction for their neighbors. Thanks to Mr. Kennedy's connections, the basement was outfitted with a movie screen and a sound projector. On Fridays, the family invited friends over to see the latest films.

It is hard to imagine now, but when Jack Kennedy turned ten, motion pictures were still silent. Then, in the fall of 1927, with the debut of a film called *The Jazz Singer*, movies started to talk. It was exciting enough for most families just to go to a movie theater and be able to watch actors moving—talking!—on the screen. The town of Hyannis didn't have a sound theater until 1929. So being able to show talking movies in one's very own home probably seemed like something akin to magic.

It must have been strange and exciting for Jack to know that his father was in the movie business. Then, like today, the name Hollywood conjured up images of glamour and fame, and the Kennedy children felt

some of the glitter rubbing off on them. It was a trade-off that came with having to be separated from their dad.

Despite his long absences, Mr. Kennedy made sure he stayed in touch. He called on Sundays, and the children lined up in order of age to speak to him. They were encouraged to write him letters; even Rosemary and the younger children just learning to print wrote about what they were doing. Mr. Kennedy would respond on the same day he received their notes, describing the movies he was making and praising the children for getting good grades and being helpful to their mother. As always, Joe Jr. was expected to set the example in that regard, and in May of 1929 he had to step in for his father during an unhappy occasion.

While Mr. Kennedy was in Hollywood, having recently returned there from a trip home, his father, P.J. Kennedy, died. Unable to make it back in time for the funeral, Joe Kennedy asked his eldest son to go in his place. Thirteen-year-old Joe Jr. exceeded his father's expectations for poise and performance, and Mr. Kennedy wrote to praise and thank him.

> *I want to tell you of the lovely reports I got from Boston about you at Grandpa's funeral. Everybody says you . . . handled yourself splendidly. I was terribly disappointed not to be there myself, but I was more than proud to have you there as my own representative and delighted everybody liked you so much. . . . I want to take this opportunity to congratulate you on the splendid record you have made this year at school. Your making up those subjects was a real worthwhile achievement, and while we have had a little disagreement once in a while about some particular thing, I am very proud of your efforts and results. . . . help mother and everybody out as much as you can and I will be with you as soon as possible.*

The Kennedy children were not only in constant communication with their father, they also received messages from some of his new employees—real-live Hollywood movie stars. When Jack and Joe came down with the measles, they received a telegram from Tom Mix, a cowboy star who rode across the silver screen on his equally famous horse, Tony: "Had them myself and I know how miserable they can be. Visit me in California and I will give you a horse and a complete outfit."

The boys didn't go to Hollywood, but Tom Mix did send them cowboy hats and chaps, just like the ones he wore in the movies. The boys immediately dressed up in their outfits and showed them off to envious friends.

Mr. Kennedy also made the boys feel connected to his work by asking for their suggestions on new film projects. Joe Jr. spent part of one summer at camp and thought it might be fun to put some of the campers' antics in a cartoon, starring the popular comic-strip character Krazy Kat. His father agreed that this was an excellent idea. From Hollywood, he wrote his son that he was giving the project the go-ahead. Mr. Kennedy also hired football star Red Grange, nicknamed the Galloping Ghost, for a gridiron movie, thanks in part to Jack and Joe's enthusiasm for the player.

Clearly, the Kennedy family was becoming ever more glamorous and growing ever more wealthy. Nevertheless, Joe and Rose Kennedy made it a practice never to discuss money around their children, feeling that there were always more interesting things to talk about. With all their advantages, the children must have been aware that they were privileged in ways other people were not. Still, Rose wanted her children to know, as she put it, "the value of money, the foolishness of squandering it, and the painful consequences of heedless extravagance." Money, Rose emphasized, brought responsibility. She quoted the Gospel of Saint Luke to the children, "To whom much has been given, much will be required."

The children were given small allowances, out of which they were expected to buy Christmas and birthday presents for members of their family. If they needed more money, a case had to be made for it. That's exactly what Jack did at age ten when he decided he needed a larger allowance. He wrote a letter to his father, marshaling his arguments for

THE
EARLY
YEARS

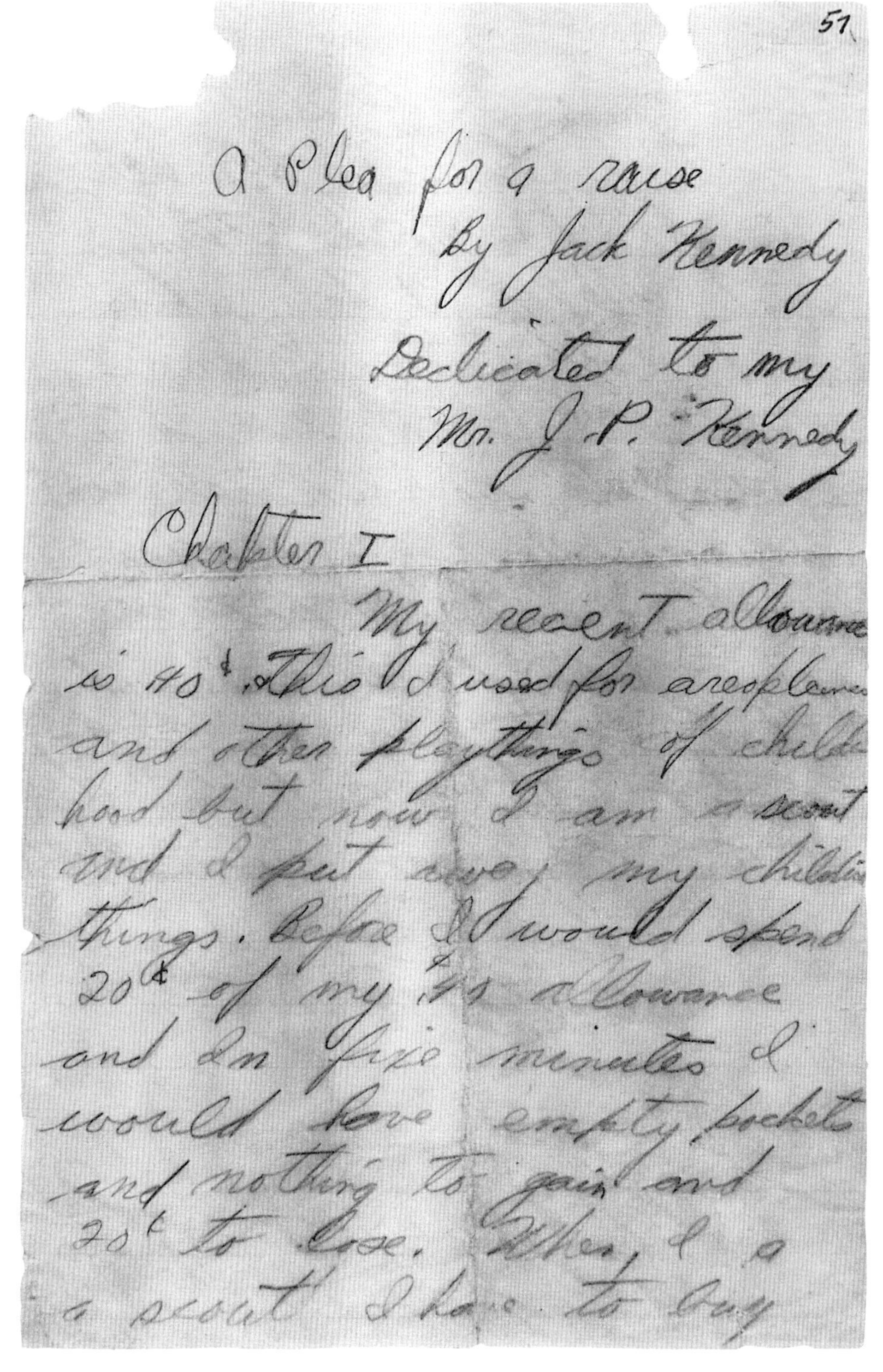

51

A Plea for a raise
By Jack Kennedy
Dedicated to my
Mr. J. P. Kennedy

Chapter I

My recent allowance is 40¢. This I used for areoplanes and other playthings of childhood but now I am a scout and I put away my childish things. Before I would spend 20¢ of my ¢.40 allowance and In five minutes I would have empty pockets and nothing to gain and 20¢ to lose. When I a a scout I have to buy

"A Plea for a raise," written by Jack Kennedy, age ten

canteens, haversacks, blankets
searchlidgs poncho things
that will last for years
and I can always use it
while I cant use a
cholcolate marshmellow
sunday with vanilla ice
cream and so I put in
my plea for a raise of
thirty cents for me to buy
scout things and pay my
own way more around.

Finis

John Fitzgerald Francis
Kennedy

extra spending money. He titled it "A Plea for a raise," and it is reproduced here, complete with spelling errors.

A Plea for a raise

By Jack Kennedy
Dedicated to my
Mr. J.P. Kennedy

Chapter I

My recent allowance is 40¢. This I used for areoplanes and other playthings of childhood but now I am a scout and I put away my childish things. Before I would spend 20¢ of my $.40 allowance and In fixe [five] minutes I would have empty pockets and nothing to gain and 20¢ to lose. When I am a scout I have to buy canteens, haversacks, blankets searchlidgs [searchlights] poncho things that will last for years and I can always use it while I cant use a chol-colate marshmellow sunday with vanilla ice cream and so I put in my plea for a raise of thirty cents for me to buy scout things and pay my own way more around.

Finis
John Fitzgerald Francis Kennedy

Mrs. Kennedy noted many years later that she had no idea why Jack included the name Francis in his signature—it wasn't part of his given name—except perhaps to remind his father of gentle St. Francis, and so help his cause. Mr. and Mrs. Kennedy must have been impressed by Jack's "plea"—they saved it along with other important family mementos. They also raised his allowance, a tribute to Jack's powers of persuasion.

“THE BOY WHO DOESN’T GET THINGS DONE”

CHAPTER VII

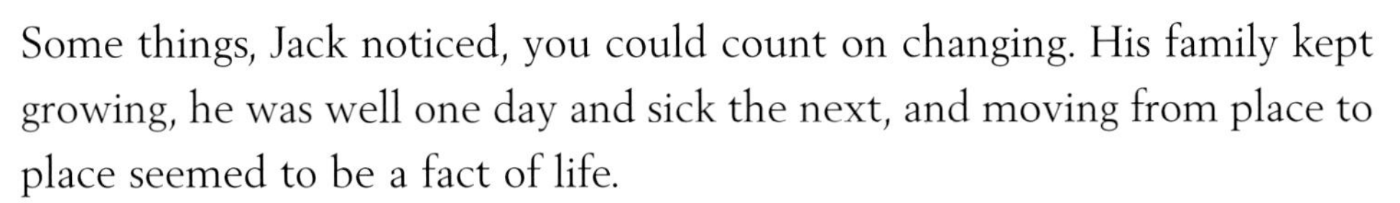

Some things, Jack noticed, you could count on changing. His family kept growing, he was well one day and sick the next, and moving from place to place seemed to be a fact of life.

In the summer of 1928, the Kennedys had been in their rented house in Riverdale for almost a year, though the search continued for a nearby home that they could purchase. They finally found it on Pondfield Road in nearby Bronxville, New York, a pretty village located a few miles north of Riverdale. Bronxville had one of the highest per capita incomes in the country, so it’s not surprising that Mr. Kennedy paid the then-astounding sum of $250,000 (at least $2.5 million today) for the family’s largest and most lavish house yet. Called Crownlands, it was a huge redbrick Colonial-style dwelling whose outside entrance was studded with large white columns. The house, set on six carefully groomed acres, boasted twenty bedrooms, more than enough for the family, the servants, visiting relatives, and assorted other guests.

Jack and Joe remained at Riverdale Country School, where they were

THE EARLY YEARS

Jack (right) and Joe Jr. with their father around the time the family moved to Bronxville, New York

now more comfortable. Despite any lingering problems over their religion, both boys had become quite popular. Each brother drew to himself a loyal gang of friends. Joe's pals were the boys who wanted to shine. Jack's buddies were the kids looking for a good time.

Girls were starting to figure into their lives as well. The brothers were invited to boy-girl parties, like the costume party where Joe went as a pirate, and Jack, a prince. Joe Jr. liked girls and vice versa. Jack, however, was so shy with the opposite sex that he refused to talk to girls on the telephone. Instead of attending his dance classes, he hid in the bathroom.

The Kennedy house in Bronxville, so large and inviting, became the place their friends wanted to hang out. Joe Jr., Jack, and Kathleen had the third floor to themselves. Between the boys' bedrooms and Kathleen's was an enormous playroom stocked with board games like Parcheesi and checkers and decks of cards for hard-fought games of hearts. For a change of pace, there was also a record player and all the latest records for the kids to listen to. The touch-football games played at Hyannis Port were a regular feature in Bronxville, too. Jack and his siblings tried to include Rosemary in the fun. Even though she was not athletic enough to play with outsiders, she was made referee.

Jack was eleven when the Kennedys moved to Bronxville, on the brink of his teenage years, and at a place in his life where he began to have a clearer idea of his family's complicated dynamics. As he got older, he seemed to grow tired of the head-to-head aspect of his competition with Joe. Whether consciously or unconsciously, Jack slowly began to adopt his brother, one observer put it, as "a role model in reverse." Joe was careful and deliberate, so Jack acted more recklessly. Joe was serious about his studies; Jack's attitude was decidedly casual. Joe was hot-tempered; Jack was reserved and cool. And lacking the pressure that was put on Joe as the eldest son, Jack had the luxury of being much more lighthearted. As one family biographer said, Joe may have been the model child, but Jack was the "Pied Piper," the quick, witty brother who led the younger

Kennedys down a merry path. If Joe Jr. impressed the younger children with his authority and wooed them by coaching them in sports or teaching them to sail, Jack captivated his siblings with his happy-go-lucky attitude toward life and his mischievous sense of humor. As he made his way into his teenage years, he managed to forge a special relationship with each of them.

To Rosemary, Jack was a protector. Along with Joe and especially Eunice, he watched out for his sister and made sure that whatever activity the children were up to, she was safe and secure. Although Rosemary was not mentally quick, she could appreciate a simple joke, and Jack liked to make her laugh. He took her out to crew on his boat, and when they started going to dances, he sometimes went down to her school in Rhode Island just to be her escort.

The younger girls—Eunice, Pat, and Jean—admired and looked up to Jack. Pat described her older teenage brothers as "young gods." Eunice said, "We yearned to please them and be acceptable. Not that any of us

The Kennedy family, including dog Buddy, in front of their Hyannis Port home, circa 1929. From left to right: Bobby, Jack (kneeling), Eunice, Jean, Mr. Kennedy, Mrs. Kennedy, Patricia, Kathleen, Joe Jr. (sitting), and Rosemary.

would necessarily show it any overt way." She also remembered Jack as the one in the family who "liked to look things up." The girls loved spending time with Jack, whether it was being allowed to play on his touch-football team or just to stand next to him while the family sang around the piano. Once, when a family friend told Eunice that she looked like Jack, Jean asked who she looked like. When she was told "Bobby," she argued bitterly. She wanted to look like Jack, too.

Jack was also something of a hero to Bobby. Baby Teddy, the Kennedy's ninth and last child, was not born until 1932, so when the family moved to Bronxville, Bobby was the only boy besides Joe and Jack. Eight years younger than Jack, stuck among a batch of sisters, four older and one younger, Bobby was the runt of the litter. His mother worried he might be "a sissy." As Bobby got older, Joe Jr. was determined to make the little boy fearless. He would do things like take Bobby out boating in stormy weather or order him to dive off boards so high Mrs. Kennedy had to close her eyes rather than watch. Despite all the time Joe Jr. spent with Bobby, though, it was Jack who won his heart. Not yet in kindergarten, Bobby would wait eagerly for Jack to come home from school. Then they would take long walks, during which Jack would regale his younger brother with tales of high adventure, like the stories about King Arthur and his Round Table that he now knew by heart.

Of all his siblings, however, it was Kathleen to whom Jack felt the closest. Almost three years younger than Jack, Kathleen was as witty and devilish as he was. Everyone called her "Kick," and the nickname captured her high spirits and love of life. She was petite like her mother, and resembled her, but she had her father's fair coloring. Mr. Kennedy had to admit that Kathleen was his favorite daughter. Though he noted, "all my ducks are swans," he said Kick was "especially special." Kathleen was not the prettiest of the Kennedy sisters, but she was the one everybody remembered. Good at sports, ready to take any dare, an all-around excellent companion, Kathleen was adored not just by Jack, but also by Joe Jr.

Because she was close to both her brothers, she became a link between them.

Jack was probably pleased that he was carving out a place in his family that was quite different from Joe's. He was also smart enough to realize that all the attention directed at his brother meant less focus on him, which had its advantages. Considering his bad habits and his inattention to school subjects in which he had no interest, Jack had to figure that perhaps it was best if his parents' eyes were on Joe. He also was coming to a realization about why he insisted on being Joe's opposite. As he said some years later, "My brother is the efficient one in the family, and I'm the boy who doesn't get things done. . . . If my brother were not so efficient, it would be easier for me. . . . He does it so much better than I do."

The years at Riverdale were good ones for Jack. His health stabilized and even his grades improved. In the sixth grade, he got a 97 in history and he won the school competition for best essay. But those days were

Jack's best pal in the family, Kathleen (fourth from the left), took on the role of eldest sister, since Rosemary (standing behind her) was unable to do so.

coming to a close. Mr. and Mrs. Kennedy decided it was time to start sending the older children off to boarding school. Mr. Kennedy, determined that the boys go to college at his alma mater, Harvard, thought they'd have the best chance of getting in if they spent their high-school years at a prestigious boarding school.

Mrs. Kennedy was more interested in travel than ever—she was to make seventeen trips to Europe in the next seven years. The younger children could stay at home supervised by nannies, but she wanted the older children in schools where their days would be regimented, with adult eyes on them at all times. She was particularly worried about Kathleen, who, as she grew older, was becoming a magnet for boys. Mrs. Kennedy frowned on the male attention that Kick received, and she decided that an all-girl Catholic boarding school would be the best place for her daughter.

The first child to go away, however, was Joe. The headmaster at Riverdale considered him one of the "best boys," with "scholastic aptitude high above average." He wanted Joe to stay right where he was. But Mr. Kennedy had decided to enroll Joe Jr. at Choate, an all-male boarding school in Wallingford, Connecticut, where he would rub shoulders with the sons of New England's socially elite families.

It was a difficult transition for fourteen-year-old Joe. In September

Kennedy, John
RIVERDALE COUNTRY SCHOOL
Upper School Scholarship Report
Form IA for period ending Feb 25, 1930

SUBJECTS:		
Chemistry		
Civics		
Drawing		
English		C 3
French		D 3
General Science		
Geography		A 1
German		
Greek		
History		
Latin		
Manual Training		
Mathematics		B+ 2
Music		
Penmanship	B 2	
Physiology		
Physics		
Average		C+

Absence 2 Demerits

Creditable, Jack 75+
Now for Honors
Head Master.

(over)

A mid-semester report card for Jack during his last year at Riverdale Country School. He was a C+ student during his final semester. The next year, he would be at boarding school.

of 1929, with his parents away in Europe, Joe arrived at Choate alone. Within a matter of hours and a couple of hundred miles, he went from being top dog at home to a school where freshmen, called third formers, had to take plenty of teasing—and worse—before they could even begin to get any recognition.

Jack heard about the older boys hazing his brother, and he was delighted. In a letter to his father, he wrote that Joe had been caught roughhousing by a sixth former who, along with some friends, decided to teach him a lesson. "All the sixth formers had a swat or two. Did the sixth formers lick him! O man, he was all blisters, they almost paddled the life out of him." Satisfaction oozing across the page, Jack added enviously, "What I wouldn't have given to be a sixth former."

Adding insult to his apparently real injuries, Joe started out poorly in his studies at Choate. Early in his first term, his mother received a letter from the school saying that Joe was at the bottom of his class. Mrs. Kennedy wrote the headmaster, Mr. George St. John, that she was sure Joe would change his ways, "as he [has] never been satisfied to have a low standing in his class."

When Joe Jr. came home for the Thanksgiving holiday in November 1929, Jack finally saw a chink in his brother's armor. He wrote to Mr. Kennedy, who was off in Hollywood, that Joe was full of "bull." Jack seemed to gloat as he recounted how "when Joe came home he was telling me how strong he was, and how tough. The first thing he did to show me how tough he was to get sick so that he could not have any Thanksgiving dinner. Manly youth. He was then going to show me how to Indian wrestle. I then through [threw] him over my neck."

But if Jack thought Joe was about to fall off his pedestal, he was soon to be disappointed. Typically, Joe buckled down at Choate and began doing well—making decent grades, joining the football team, and gaining the respect of his fellow students. Jack stayed at Riverdale for the rest of the school year. Then, in the fall of 1930, his eighth-grade year, he, too, joined the ranks of boarding-school students. There was talk of Jack going to Choate, but Mr. Kennedy was away in Hollywood, and Rose decided at the last moment that perhaps there was a chance for Jack to get some Catholic education after all.

She chose a school called Canterbury in the foothills near New Milford, Connecticut. The school buildings surrounded a stone church, all high on a bluff; the stark setting was not very welcoming. Nevertheless, thirteen-year-old Jack signed in with ninety-two other new students who came from as far away as Tennessee, Illinois, and Utah.

Years later, asked if he had wanted to go to boarding school, Jack answered, "No." But without any say in the matter, he did what was expected of him. His parents were pleased with the way Joe had settled into his new school environment. Now it was Jack's turn to find out what it was like to live away from home.

HOMESICK

CHAPTER VIII

"It's a pretty good place, but I was pretty homesick the first night. The swimming pool is great even if the football team looks pretty bad. You have a whole lot of religion and the studies are pretty hard. The only time you get out of here is to see the Harvard–Yale and the Yale and Army [games]. This place is freezing at night and pretty cold in the daytime."

Jack wrote lots of letters home while he was at Canterbury. Perhaps it was because he was homesick—or maybe the school required regular communication with parents. In any case, he wrote about a variety of topics: his grades, his activities, his health, his faith. His correspondence showed an originality of thought, an amusing way of looking at things, and an almost total disregard for spelling. His letters also showed that he was growing up.

For one thing, he had a new interest in his appearance. Soon after arriving at Canterbury, Jack wrote to his mother, "Send me up a gray pair of pants like Joe's please, and I can wear them with my blue coat and new black shoes and then I will be able to get fitted for a gray suit next time in N.Y." When his mother ignored his request and sent a suit instead, he returned it with a note informing her he didn't like the color and "it was pretty itchy looking material."

Jack was more questioning about religion than Joe Jr. and some of his other siblings, but the religious aspect of Canterbury was also making an impression on this former St. Aiden's altar boy. Catholicism was an important part of daily life at the school. ". . . we have religious talks on Tuesday and Catacism [catechism] on Wednesday," he wrote to his parents. Jack sounds only a little tongue-in-cheek when he says that he expects to be "quite puis [pious] when I get home."

If Mrs. Kennedy was pleased that Jack was getting the Catholic education she wanted for him, she must have been taken aback to learn that theft seemed common at the school. "A lot of things have been swiped. My sweat shirt, $5.00. $1.50 worth of stamps, fountain pens, pillows and $35.00 with lots of other stuff." Nor could she be happy to learn how he was getting pummeled on the playing fields of Canterbury: "My nose, my leg and other part [parts] of my anatomy have been risked around so much that it is beginning to be funny," he reported in another letter.

On a less dangerous front, Jack informed his parents, "I learnt how to play baggamon [backgammon] to-day. . . ." Playing bridge was another pleasurable activity. He tried out for the choir, but that didn't go very well. The teacher asked him to sing: ". . . he asked me to go OO oooo I went ~~OO!~~ ~~xxx~~ so he thought I was only fooling and he said so. . . . My voice must be changing because when I go up it sounds as if Buddy [the family dog] were howling. I go up another note and Buddy is choking, another and Buddy and me have gasped our last."

CANTERBURY SCHOOL
NEW MILFORD, CONNECTICUT

Record of John Kennedy, Form II
From November 1 to December 6, 1930.

Any average from 90% to 100% is accounted "Very Good"; from 80% to 90% "Good"; from 70% to 80% "Fair"; from 60% to 70% "Poor"; and below 60% "Unsatisfactory".

SUBJECT	DAILY WORK	EFFORT AND APPLICATION	FORM AVERAGE
English II	86	Good	71.69
Latin II	55	Poor	64.35
History II	77	Good	67.00
Mathematics II	95	Good	61.69
Science II	72	Good	66.62
Religion II	75	Fair	78.46
AVERAGE: 77.00			

This report is not quite so good as the last one. The damage was done chiefly by "Poor" effort in Latin, in which Jack got a mark of 55. He can do better than this. In fact, his average should be well in the 80's.

N.H.

This report card reflects Jack's appreciation of English, his lack of effort in Latin (as his teacher's note comments upon), and a surprisingly high mark in math.

Scholastically, things got off to a good start for Jack. He wrote to his parents during his first semester that his grades were in the mid-90s with a few more in the 80s and 70s. And though Jack said his science class was hard, he earned a 90 in it. He also got an 80 in history. As the year wore on, a low grade in Latin, a 68, pulled him down. Latin was the bane of Jack's existence. His struggles with gender, cases, and declension and with the teacher's tough grading led him to vow in a letter, "It wont be this month and maybe not next but I am going to pass Latin for at least one month . . ." Not only did he lack an aptitude for the ancient language, he seemed plagued with bad luck when it came to the subject. On one test, he was the last student to hand in his paper. The teacher mixed up Jack's test with some corrected papers, and then, over Jack's heated protests, maintained that Jack had never handed it in. To Jack's indignation, the teacher gave him a zero. As he wrote his parents, "What a mess!"

His best subject, as always, was English. The class was reading his favorite author, Sir Walter Scott, who wrote about knights and battles, so Jack did

CANTERBURY SCHOOL
NEW MILFORD, CONNECTICUT

I certainly was glad Eddie came up though Kathleen sent my a valentine signed Mary Thompson but she forgot that Mary Thompson did not live in Bronxville and I saw the post-mark addressed Bronxville

Pat, Bobby Eunice and Kick have all sent me letters and ~~Rat~~ Pat Eunice and Kick sent me valentines. I got your letter to-day. Mother, the temperature reached something like 55° here so I guess

A letter from Canterbury. The "Eddie" Jack refers to in his letter is his father's friend Eddie Moore. Sir Walter Scott, author of "The Lady of the Lake," was one of Jack's favorite writers.

particularly well. He used his standing in English class both to boast about his grades and to cover his tracks on some of the bad habits his mother was always riding him about: "Though I may not be able to remember where I put material things such as tickets, gloves, and so on I can remember things like Ivanhoe and the last time we had a test on it, I got a ninety-eight."

More important than any book learning Jack acquired at Canterbury was his growing sensitivity to the often inexplicable twists and turns of life. His own unpredictable health, along with Rosemary's struggles, must already have made Jack feel keenly how unfair life could sometimes be. But now that he was a teenager, events beyond his own needs and pleasures began to penetrate his awareness.

In October 1929, just a few months after Mr. Kennedy paid a quarter of a million dollars for the house in Bronxville, the stock market crashed. On a day known as "Black Tuesday," stocks owned by individuals, banks, corporations, and pension funds plunged in value, creating an economic disaster that led to America's Great Depression in the 1930s. Many

you havent anything
on me. We also have
swimming though
I can only swim once
a week. You have
golf, we have basketball
skating and squash.
I learnt how to
play baggamon to-day
and in learning I
got licked both games

but I hope to
improve. That
is about all though
my Latin could stand
improving
Lots of
Love,
Jack
P.S. We
have Scott's
Lady of the
Lake in
English

wealthy people had their fortunes wiped out. Average wage earners across the country lost their jobs and found themselves unable to provide for their families.

The tough economic times did not touch Joseph P. Kennedy. Mr. Kennedy was shrewd about the ways of the stock market. Sensing that many stocks were overvalued and heading for a tumble, he sold his holdings just before the crash, leaving him richer than ever.

As an adult, Jack said his family's standard of living actually rose during the Depression. So perhaps it's no surprise that he was unaware of the crash until 1930. Once Jack learned about the country's worsening financial situation, he wanted to know what the stock-market crash was all about and how it affected people. He wrote to his father for information and said, "Please send me the Literary Digest [a magazine] because I did not know about the Market Slump." He also asked for a newspaper subscription, which furthered his interest in current events. Jack was an avid newspaper reader for the rest of his life.

At a more personal level, Jack was disturbed by a tobogganing accident in which one of his friends was seriously injured. The vivid description of it in a letter he wrote home captures the feelings of a boy trying to come to terms with tragedy and with the vulnerabilities of flesh and blood.

> *[He was] lyi[ng?] on the ground holding his stoma[ch?]. We lifted him up, he began to faint and so we put him on my sled and towed him . . . up a hill, and then . . . to school. He was all gray and as we carried him up stairs, he fainted. He went to the hospital a hour later and he was just ~~as~~ a white grayish color. I think maybe he was operated on yesterday but I am not sure. He had internal ~~injury~~ injuries and I liked him a ~~lote~~ lot.*

What Jack didn't know was that soon he would be the one going into the hospital. At Canterbury, his health took a downward turn almost as soon as he arrived. He began losing weight, and his vision became blurry. He wrote indignantly to his parents that the other boys were teasing him about his "delicay" (delicacy).

> *It is not much fun taking a rest because it breaks up my basket ball by half. Also with my milk and crackers I cannot have any tea because I have to take them at recess. That with my tonic results in recieving some kidding about my delicay though I suppose that does not make any difference it is not exactly comfortable. I am made out to be an awful baby. About my eye I did speak to you in vacation about it and you said you would have me examined the next time I came to the dentist. It has gotten worse and everything is a blur at over eight feet but if you ~~do~~ want me to wait till Easter I will if you think it best. I just saw Mrs. Hume and the doctor is coming to see me because my face has grown red from top to bottom and is very not [hot].*
>
> *My knees are very red with white lumps of skin but I guess I will pull through.*
>
> *Love*
> *Jack*

Having people notice his weak constitution was surely unpleasant for Jack. His mother once said, "Jack went along for many years thinking to himself—or at least trying to make others think—that he was a strong, robust quite healthy person who happened to be sick a good deal of the time." Just as winning was extolled in the Kennedy house, illness was frowned upon. The Kennedy children were expected to ignore sickness as best they could; if you did have to stay in bed, you didn't linger there. Eunice, who had some of the same maladies as her brother, including an easily upset stomach, remembered being discouraged from thinking of herself as sickly. "My mother sent everybody outdoors because she wanted everybody to be healthy and robust. It didn't matter if you were a little sick . . . you took care of yourself and then you hustled right along."

Jack's stomach problems, backaches, and periods of fatigue were embarrassing for him, as well as serving as strong reminders of how he differed from the hardy Joe. It was one thing to have a special place in the family because he was the intellectual. It was quite another to be known as the sickly brother.

In later years, Mrs. Kennedy would say that she and her husband "were accustomed to the idea that every now and then [Jack] would be laid up by some disease or accident." Rose added, "what concerned us as much, or more, was his lack of diligence in his studies." That sentiment must have been unsettling to Jack. Did his parents really care more about his grades than his health?

Surprisingly, his frequent bouts of illness did not lead Jack into self-pity or bring his spirits down, at least not in ways that were obvious. If anything, they seemed to hone his wit and sense of irony. Jack was always underplaying his bad health, and he did so with humor. He frequently joked about his aching body parts, and as a teenager, he and a friend decided that if a biography was ever written about him it should be entitled *John F. Kennedy: A Medical History.* He often repeated Bobby's quip: mosquitoes that bit his brother would quickly die, having sucked up some of Jack Kennedy's blood. Jack learned an important truth early—sometimes the only way to deal with trouble is to laugh at it.

But now, in a chilly, drafty old school, away from home for the first time since he had been hospitalized with scarlet fever as a toddler, Jack became sicker than he had been in a while, and it was scary. It started with a bad case of hives: ". . . that is a sickness which everything begins to itch. My face ~~had~~ hands knees and feet. . . . The icheting [itching] is ferocious and it is hard to sleep. The doctor up here just painted it ~~whith~~ with idione [iodine] and that has done no good. . . . It is spreding [spreading] ~~for~~ from the bottom of my chin to my cheeks to my head."

Jack (right) and Joe Jr. with their father in Palm Beach, Florida

As alarming as that description sounds, worse was to come. During a talk by a missionary from India—"one of the most interesting talks that I ever heard"—Jack felt himself grow dizzy and weak. "I just about fainted and everything began to grow black," he wrote home, "so I went out and then I fell and Mr. Hume [the headmaster] caught me. I'm O.K. now." Jack added that since Joe Jr. had fainted twice in church, "I guess I will live."

The hives and dizzy spell were the first symptoms of a spiral downward. Jack began to have trouble concentrating, he would get unexplained fevers, and he felt exhausted. He couldn't even get his weight up enough to be allowed to swim.

Mr. and Mrs. Kennedy thought an Easter break in Florida might help restore his health and spirits. The economic situation brought about by the collapse of the stock market may have been devastating for the rest of the country, but Joe Kennedy had recently purchased a Spanish-style villa on North Ocean Drive in Palm Beach for the family's winter vacations. The house, which cost over $100,000 (more than a million dollars today) featured a red-tiled living room that opened onto the ocean. Jack did seem to feel better after the rest and relaxation, but back at Canterbury, he collapsed once again, this time with stomach pains. Rushed to a nearby hospital, he underwent an emergency appendectomy. The operation was a standard one, but Jack did not recover as quickly as most patients. By May, he still was not well enough to return to Canterbury. So, in conjunction with the school, his parents decided that he would go home and be tutored for final exams there.

Between his early homesickness and his variety of ailments, Jack's stay at Canterbury had been trying; even his mother admitted it was not his most successful year. But bigger challenges lay ahead. The Kennedys had decided that the next stage of Jack's education would take place at the top-notch boarding school Choate. And once again, Joe had gotten there first.

"QUITE DIFFERENT FROM JOE"

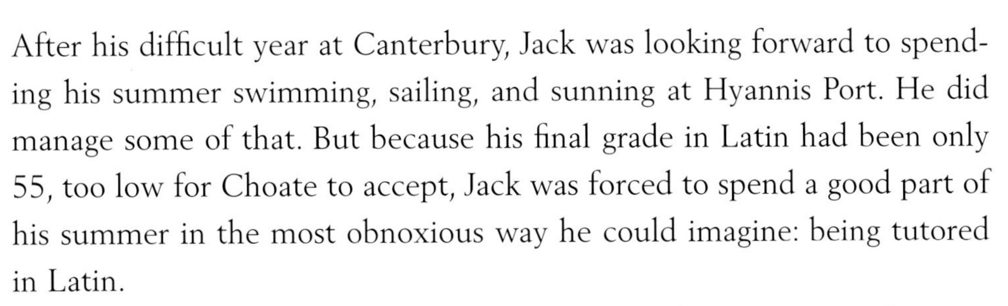

CHAPTER IX

After his difficult year at Canterbury, Jack was looking forward to spending his summer swimming, sailing, and sunning at Hyannis Port. He did manage some of that. But because his final grade in Latin had been only 55, too low for Choate to accept, Jack was forced to spend a good part of his summer in the most obnoxious way he could imagine: being tutored in Latin.

The headmaster at Choate, Mr. George St. John, was sympathetic to Jack's plight. As he explained in a letter to Jack's parents, he understood that Jack did well in subjects like history and English, where his imagination could soar, and that he disliked subjects with lots of rules, like foreign languages and math. But Mr. St. John wasn't going to make any exceptions to Choate's entry requirements. Jack would have to pass a Latin examination in the fall. He wrote to Rose, "I guess Jack will simply have to work on this job as one that just has to be done."

Despite Jack's troubles with Latin, the headmaster probably imagined that Jack was a boy like Joe: one who might start out slowly but would apply himself, work hard, and make Choate proud. Little did Mr. St. John know that he and rest of his staff were about to spend the next four years fighting with Jack Kennedy about everything from his grades to his attitude to the condition of his room. It was a fight Jack seemed to relish.

Rose Kennedy, suspecting that Mr. St. John might be harboring hopes of another Joe Jr., cautiously wrote to the headmaster the summer before Jack entered Choate: "[Jack] has a very attractive personality, we think, but he is quite different from Joe for whom we feel you have done so much."

It was true that Joe had blossomed at Choate. After a shaky start, he had gone on to become one of the "best boys ever," according to one of his teachers. Now about to be a fifth former, the equivalent of a high-school junior, Joe was well regarded by both the staff and his fellow students. He was on the football team, a member of the student council, and worked on the yearbook. He belonged to the Andrews Society, a club that did good works for charity. As Mr. St. John wrote to the Kennedys, Joe is a boy "on whom we are going to depend."

"Joe did many things well," Jack noted later. Yet he seemed to need his parents' reassurance that he was following the path laid out for him. Joe regularly wrote home about his course work ("I have to work pretty hard though most courses are interesting") and how he was doing in football: "I was not in the first team line-up, but after about the first three minutes of the first quarter the coach sent me in for right-end, and I played there until the last two minutes of the game." In a bit of irony Joe probably didn't catch, he painstakingly detailed how he was spending every bit of his allowance (20 cents church, 50 cents haircut, 15 cents ice cream) yet just a week later, he excitedly informed Mr. Kennedy about a brochure he had solicited from a yacht broker, who had an "excellent buy" on a boat—much better than another craft he was looking at for $1200.

Still, there were flashes of self-awareness. As a staff member of the school yearbook, one of Joe's jobs was to write some jokes for it. He ruefully admitted in a letter home that "I am not very good thinking up wise-cracks," perhaps remembering that he had a brother who was known for his wit. He even dared to challenge his mother and her habits: "Received your letter to-day. I can easily understand how busy you must be buying antiques and clothes." This bit of sarcasm was practically unheard of for Joe. His letters were usually shining examples of the sort of correspondence parents love to receive: full of news about his churchgoing and good grades and interested inquiries about his younger siblings.

During the summer of 1931, as Jack was struggling with his Latin books, Joe Jr. received a singular honor. Russell Boardman, the pilot of the aircraft *Cape Cod,* was coming to town, and Joe had been chosen to escort him around. Boardman had recently made what was then the longest flight in history, from Brooklyn, New York, to Istanbul, Turkey—5,500 miles in forty-nine hours. The town of Hyannis staged a parade with sixty floats and six marching bands; thousands came from around the area to cheer the hero. At the head of the festivities was Joe Kennedy Jr., driving his father's Rolls-Royce and chatting with Boardman, who sat next to him. Jack must have looked on with envy.

As he contemplated his new school, Jack no doubt asked Joe questions about Choate. Although Canterbury and Choate were both in Connecticut, only twenty-five miles apart, Jack had never visited Joe. Choate had a look and feel that was very different from Spartan Canterbury. Choate's spacious, tree-lined campus was nestled among rolling hills in the town of Wallingford. Along with playing fields for football and baseball, there were eighteen tennis courts, stables, and a new gym big enough for hockey. Choate also had an infirmary, a place Jack would come to know all too well.

Like all the schools Jack had attended since Devotion, the students at Choate came from well-to-do families, and like all the schools except for Canterbury, they were overwhelmingly Protestant. No matter what their religious affiliation, however, Choate boys were required to attend a daily

Episcopalian service in the stately wood-paneled school chapel. After chapel on Sunday, the few Catholic students went into the town of Wallingford for Mass.

Choate promised parents "efficient teaching, manly discipline, systematic exercise, and association with boys of purpose." The rules were strict and the classwork was difficult. Students were expected to maintain high standards, both academically and socially—demonstrating courtesy, fair play, and good behavior. Choate boys were supposed to be a credit to their school at all times, in preparation for becoming upstanding citizens and future leaders.

It was into this highly structured, highly traditional atmosphere that a tall, very skinny, fourteen-year-old Jack Kennedy arrived as a third former, or freshman. His first act on campus was to lose the piece of paper that told him where to take the Latin exam he needed to pass in order to gain entrance. His mother had to cable him with the information.

Perhaps because his teeth protruded slightly in his thin face, Jack was almost immediately tagged with the nickname "Ratface." It was given in good fun, however, and before long, Jack had found a group of friends to pal around with.

"Everyone likes your boy," Mrs. St. John, the headmaster's wife, wrote to Mrs. Kennedy during the first month of school, "and he is rapidly making a real place for himself in the life of the school."

This good impression of Jack faded fast, at least among the staff. Many of the boys lived in small frame houses scattered around the campus, and Jack had been assigned to live in one called School House. The housemaster, Earl "Cap" Leinbach, was a World War I hero who had escaped a German firing squad. Personable and interested in his charges, he was one of the best-liked teachers on campus. Jack liked Cap, too, but that didn't mean he was about to change his habits for him.

"Jack has a pleasing personality, and is warmly received by all the boys in the house, but rules bother him a bit," Cap noted with understatement in his first report about Jack.

"QUITE DIFFERENT FROM JOE"

As Jack entered his teenage years, despite his messy habits, he liked to look sharp.

Cap saw Jack breaking one particular rule daily: students were expected to keep their rooms neat and tidy. Jack's clothes were tossed in a heap and his books were scattered all over the floor. Wadded-up papers missed the wastepaper basket more often than they landed inside. Jack's sloppiness soon began to grate on his roommate, a boy named Godfrey, who couldn't stand living with such a slob. The messier the room became, the angier Godfrey got; that's when the fighting started. Finally the boys divided the room in half. The demarcation line was a small rug: Godfrey kept his things on one side, Jack let his stuff pile up like garbage on the other.

The rug didn't solve the problem, because the rule said every room was to be kept neat—both sides. Cap kept after Jack about tidiness. In one report he wrote, "Whenever Jack wants a clean shirt or a suit, it is necessary for him to pull every shirt or suit out of the drawer and then he 'does not have time to put them back.' His room is inspected night and morning, and I always find the floor cluttered with articles of every description." Cap added that a good-natured Jack would start to stuff everything back in the drawers once Cap entered the room, often remarking, "I never get away with anything in this place."

This habit of dropping clothes everywhere led to lots of dry-cleaning bills, and that caught Mr. Kennedy's attention. In a letter to Jack, he wrote with displeasure about a $10.80 bill for "suit pressing," as much as most students spent on clothes care in a year. "It strikes me that this is very high and while I want you to keep looking well, I think that if you spent a little more time picking up your clothes instead of leaving them on the floor, it wouldn't be necessary to have them pressed so often."

Cap was also responsible for overseeing Jack's studies, and the housemaster was no more successful at coaxing good grades from Jack than he was in getting him to clean his room. Despite all the problems Jack was causing, Cap, like most people, couldn't help but like him. "What makes the whole problem more difficult is Jack's winning smile and charming personality. . . . It is an inescapable fact that his actions are really amusing and evoke hilarity."

Certainly, his classmates found his pranks amusing. His stunts were typical schoolboy mischief, short-sheeting beds or filling up a pal's room with pillows so the boy couldn't get in the door. Once, when his mother sent him a crate of oranges from Florida to improve his health, Jack used the fruit as missiles, lobbing them onto unsuspecting passersby. Another time, he stole a life-size cardboard cutout of the sexy actress Mae West from one of the local movie theaters. He put "Mae" in his bed to shock the cleaning lady.

As he settled into life at Choate, Jack made an effort to participate in school activities. He ran for president of the freshman class, along with twenty-nine other boys, but he didn't come close to winning. He also tried out for the football team, but he was too slight to make even junior varsity. The best he could do that year was play intramural football.

Choate offered no freshman history course, so except for English, Jack was stuck with subjects he disliked—French, Latin, math—and that was a prescription for disaster.

Interestingly, despite his mediocre grades, Jack was a whiz at trivia. A weekly radio quiz program called *Information Please* required quick answers on a wide range of subjects. Jack listened to the show faithfully and could answer most of the questions, astounding his friends with the scope of his knowledge.

One of his classmates, Ralph "Rip" Horton, was particularly impressed with Jack's ability to remember things and asked him how he did it. Jack told Rip that he had a trick for sharpening his memory: he would read an article, then put it down for a half hour or so and go over it in his mind. "I'll analyze the article," Jack told Rip, "and then attack it and tear it down." Unfortunately for his classwork, Jack only bothered to use this device when it came to subjects he was interested in.

During that first fall semester, Jack began to feel comfortable at

Choate, even if Choate was not feeling comfortable with him. Then, in November, he landed in the school infirmary with swollen glands. The doctor thought perhaps he had mumps, but by the time Jack was released, the doctor had decided he didn't know what was wrong after all. This illness began a string of unknown ailments that would plague Jack throughout his Choate days.

After Christmas vacation, Jack returned to school, but by January he was in the infirmary once more, again suffering with swollen glands. "Jack was looking most picturesque in a lavender bathrobe, with lavender and green pajamas and seemed to be settling in for a pleasant stay," wrote Mrs. St. John to Rose Kennedy. A week later she wrote again, saying that although Jack was no worse, he was still in the infirmary and now had added a cough to his symptoms.

Jack recovered and felt better for a couple of months, but in April he was sick yet again. With another inexplicable mumps-like swelling on his neck, he was sent back to the infirmary. The combination of poor health and poor work habits made for school reports that were dismal, especially in French and Latin. Cap tried to help by drilling him in his language vocabularies every night and working with him on algebra. He also forbade Jack to leave his room during evening study periods, but nothing seemed to do much good.

As one teacher wrote, "Jack Kennedy has a high I.Q. and is one of the most undependable boys in the third form." His French teacher despaired. "He invariably forgets his books, pencil, or paper. There is actually very little short of physical violence that I haven't tried!"

It wasn't that Jack didn't want to succeed. He would have liked to earn good grades. If nothing else, a better performance would have gotten his teachers off his back, a result fervently to be wished for. But as Mr. St. John expressed in a letter to Jack's parents, "[he] lacks the stability and the power of concentration to do a really effective job." Rose Kennedy put it another way. "Jack couldn't or wouldn't conform. He did pretty much what he wanted, rather than what the school wanted of him."

In the end, Jack failed both Latin and French. This time the consequences were worse than simply being tutored in Hyannis Port over the summer. He was ordered to attend summer school at Choate, which took place in August. Knowing his vacation would be cut short by more than a month was a real blow to Jack. He hated to miss out on time with his family and especially regretted not having a whole summer to spend with the newest member of the family, baby Teddy, the last Kennedy child.

Teddy had arrived on February 22, 1932, George Washington's birthday, so Jack suggested his brother be named for America's first president. His parents instead chose to name the baby after a family friend, Edward Moore, who, along with his wife, Mary, had always been devoted to the Kennedy children.

When Jean Kennedy had been born, twelve-year-old Joe Jr. was chosen to be her godfather. Now Jack asked to be godfather to Teddy. That didn't mean he couldn't have a laugh at the way Kennedy babies seemed to keep on coming. When friends met Jack at the Bronxville railroad station soon after Teddy's birth, he told them, "I want to stop by the house for a minute and check to see if there's anybody new in the family." He went inside, and when he came out, he said with mock horror, "By God, there is."

Jack had mixed feelings about being part of such a large family. In later years, he called it a very institutionalized sort of life, where the boys and girls were each dressed in identical clothes and children were lined up according to age to take daily doses of vita-

Feb 1932 57

THE CHOATE SCHOOL
WALLINGFORD, CONNECTICUT

Dear Mother,
It is the night before exams so I will write you Wednesday.
Lots of Love.
P.S. Can I be Godfather to the baby

Jack's request to be godfather to his baby brother Teddy. Teddy grew up to be Senator Edward M. Kennedy of Massachusetts. The original of this letter now hangs in his office.

min-rich cod-liver oil. Life was so impersonal that in Hyannis Port and Palm Beach, none of the kids had rooms of their own with their pictures on the walls or their "stuff" on shelves. With children coming and going to boarding schools and friends and visitors streaming in and out, rooms were assigned on a first-come, first-served basis. So a returning Jack would often ask his mother, "Which room do I have now?"

On the other hand, Jack really did adore his siblings, especially his favorite, Kathleen. She and Jack, who shared the same wicked sense of humor, grew even closer as teenagers. Kathleen was also attending boarding school in Connecticut. Noroton Convent of the Sacred Heart, a Catholic school, was run by nuns from an order named the Religious of the Sacred Heart. Noroton was strict. Along with Mass every morning, Kathleen was required to observe long periods of silence to help her mind focus on spiritual matters. Although she rarely had weekends free, Jack and his sister wrote to each other, telephoned when possible, and got together whenever they could. Over the holidays, they liked nothing better than to stay up late after parties, gossiping about everyone who had been there. Kathleen was so important to Jack that when, at sixteen, he started dating a girl named Olive Cawley, he informed her how important it was to make a good impression on "Kick."

The older Jack grew, the more he realized that being part of the "Kennedy clan" was both wonderful and wearing at the same time, and that to truly know how being a family member felt, one had to be on the inside. Only his brothers and sisters could understand what it was like to grow up in a family where much was given, but even more was expected. Only the other young Kennedys could know what it was like to have a mother so concerned about the details of their lives and yet so emotionally—and physically—distant. Or a father who made his children the center of his world, but who pushed them so hard it often hurt.

Considering how much time and energy Mr. Kennedy had invested in having his children turn out the way he wanted, it is interesting that he was prepared to make them financially independent adults. Toward that end, he set up a million-dollar trust fund for each one. If they refrained from smoking or drinking, they would get even more. Perhaps in his heart Mr. Kennedy knew that he didn't need to worry about controlling his children by tightly holding the purse strings. He had exercised so much influence over his children's early lives that they would always try to please him. A close family friend noted, "Every single kid was raised to think, first: What shall I do about this problem? Second: What will Dad say about my solution of it?"

So Joe Kennedy told his children he wanted them to form their own opinions and to think their own thoughts. He was especially pleased if, during one of the family's conversational free-for-alls at dinner, Joe and Jack teamed up to argue against him. He told his wife that he didn't care if they agreed with him; young people always had different ideas from their elders. The important thing was that his children stick together.

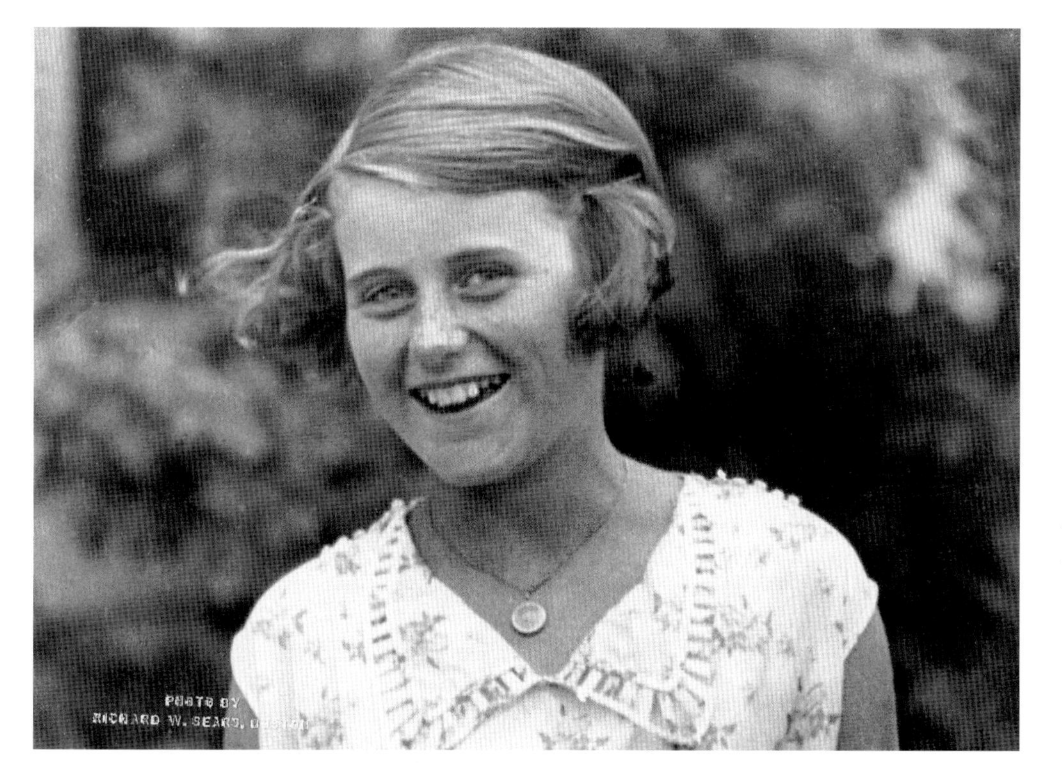

Kathleen "Kick" Kennedy at about age twelve. Fearless and funny, she was always aware that she had been born into a family of privilege and was grateful for the experiences most young people only dream of.

Rose later recalled an incident in 1935 that "emphasized my husband's deep concern about family unity." It occurred aboard the ship *Normandie,* where Mr. and Mrs. Kennedy, along with Jack and Kathleen, were sailing for Europe.

> *Lawrence Fisher, one of the famous Fisher brothers of General Motors fame, was introduced to my husband while we were enjoying a "stretch" on Deck Chairs. Immediately, we sent for Jack who was making the trip with us. When Jack came to his father's chair, hair tossed, and necktie askew from playing in a game of deck tennis, his father greeted him as follows: "Jack, I sent for you because I want you to meet Mr. Lawrence Fisher, one of the famous Fisher Body family. I wanted you to see what success brothers have who stick together."*

Despite all their rivalries, Joe and Jack did share a bond. It was forged from all sorts of things: relocations, religion, responsibility for Rosemary, and common interests like sports and a love of the sea. Both brothers knew how it felt to be the object of prejudice. Perhaps most important to their relationship was their shared memories of what it was like to grow up in the Kennedy family.

In later years, Jack's feelings would grow into respect for his brother: "He had great physical courage and stamina, a complete confidence in himself that never wavered." As teens, however, while Joe and Jack might sometimes appreciate each other and stand together against outsiders, they were not really friends. That's why Jack was so happy when, during his sophomore year at Choate, he met a boy who would become as close as a brother and his best friend as well.

JACK AND LEM

CHAPTER X

At a quick glance, Jack Kennedy and Kirk LeMoyne Billings were an unlikely duo.

Jack was tall and lithe and moved with a natural grace that was enhanced by years of swimming, tennis, and golf. Despite the Ratface nickname, with his thatch of auburn hair and his inquisitive blue-gray eyes, he was turning out to be quite good-looking. The girls who came up to Choate for dances from exclusive schools like Miss Porter's were certainly starting to pay attention.

Kirk, known as LeMoyne or Lem, was big and bulky; some people described his appearance as bearlike. He had a high forehead, a high voice, and he was clumsy. Girls didn't pay a bit of attention to him.

Unlike the "coffin-ship Kennedys," LeMoyne's ancestors had come to America on the *Mayflower.* His family had been very wealthy—then the stock market crashed and wiped out most of their fortune. Still, Lem's father was a doctor, so there was money coming into the house until Dr. Billings suddenly died, when Lem was thirteen. After that, Lem's immediate family was broke, and he had to rely on scholarships to get through Choate.

The boys met during their sophomore year while they were working on the school yearbook, *The Brief.* Jack's job was to get advertising for the yearbook, and he was a pretty good salesman, garnering more than twenty ads that year. He even managed to coax one out of the family butcher down in Palm Beach.

Almost immediately Jack and Lem became fast friends. It was easy to understand what Lem saw in Jack. Jack Kennedy was one of the most popular boys in his class, always ready with a quip or a practical joke. One classmate said, "You never knew what he was going to do next." Lem keenly appreciated the aura Jack cast. He later said about Jack: "I've never known anyone in my life with such a wonderful sense of humor, the ability to laugh and have a good time. He enjoyed things with such intensity that he made you feel whatever you were doing was absolutely the most wonderful thing you could be doing."

Lem, on the other hand, did not find it easy to make friends. He was a kid without means in a school of rich boys. He wore thick glasses that just barely allowed him to see. With his lumbering appearance and his high, slightly nasal voice, Lem was considered something of a geek.

But that wasn't the way Jack saw him. To Jack, Lem was someone he could confide in, someone who really understood him, and someone who looked up to him. Lem thought everything Jack did was great, and Jack liked knowing that somebody felt that way about him—with absolutely no reservations.

One reason Lem understood Jack so well was that Lem also had an older brother in whose shadow he stood. Frederick "Josh" Billings Jr., a recent graduate of Choate, was in many ways like Joe Jr.: a good student, a good athlete, and good-looking as well. When Jack talked about how hard it was to measure up to Joe Jr., Lem knew exactly what he meant.

From the start, their senses of humor were in sync—and as Lem noted,

Jack and Lem were lifelong friends. This picture was taken during a trip they made to Europe the summer after their graduation from Choate. Lem later remembered that he was on a tight budget, and so Jack, too, had to travel very cheaply. "He did it happily. He didn't mind at all."

"I think that's what makes two people like each other." The boys quickly invented nicknames, often puns on their names. First they were Johnny and Billy (because Lem had been a Billy Whiskers fan, too), then Ken and LeMoan. But Jack, with his witty wordplay, also made up names for Lem that had an edge to them, like Delemma and Pneumoania. Some names were not so witty. In one letter to Lem, with typical teen rudeness, Jack addressed him as "Dear Pithecanthropus, the walking ape man."

Although Jack appreciated Lem's devotion, their relationship wasn't one of equals. Jack had a large circle of friends and all the advantages that money could offer, including well-appointed vacation houses in fashionable places. Joe Jr. had started the tradition of bringing friends home for the holidays, and Jack began inviting Lem. Lem's first visit didn't go very well. He landed in the hospital for three weeks after a broken showerhead fell and doused him with scalding water.

Despite this inauspicious beginning, Lem was soon going home with Jack for most of the school holidays, spending summer vacations in Hyannis Port and winter breaks in Palm Beach. Mr. Kennedy grumbled that Lem appeared with his suitcase one day and never really left. Jack's youngest sister, Jean, said it didn't dawn on her until she was four or five that Lem wasn't just another older brother. But eventually the whole family, even Mr. Kennedy, came to love Lem, first for his loyalty to Jack and then for his own good-natured self.

As a fourth former, or sophomore, Jack had been reassigned from School House to East Cottage under the supervision of a housemaster named Eugene Musser. Despite all of his problems with Cap Leinbach, Jack had at least liked him. But he found Mr. Musser a fussy stick-in-the-mud, and not much of a challenge, either. Jack told Cap that he wished he could go back to School House. "Down where I am now, I can get away with anything and it's no fun!" Cap must have smiled to himself, since Jack's complaint when he lived at School House was that he couldn't get away with enough!

Jack and Lem having fun with Bobby beside the pool at the Kennedys' house in Palm Beach, Florida. Vacation times for Jack meant sun, relaxation, and the pleasure of being able to freely socialize with girls.

Maybe Jack didn't see Mr. Musser as a worthy opponent, but Mr. Musser soon realized what he was up against with Jack. In one of his regular reports he wrote that lack of neatness was still an issue, and he complained about Jack's "tendency to foster a gang spirit," meaning that Jack had a way of making getting into trouble look like a lot of fun.

If Jack's unwillingness—or inability—to conform persisted during his sophomore year, so, unfortunately, did his health problems. In January and February of 1933, he was once again in and out of the infirmary. First there were strange flulike symptoms. Then it was a severe pain in his knee. "Jack's winter term sounded like a hospital report," a staff member later noted. "His eyes began bothering him again" and he seemed to need attention from "the top of his head to the tips of his toes."

Despite his poor health, Jack's second year at Choate did have its high points. Although he was not strong enough to make the varsity teams, he played intramural football and baseball, astounding both coaches and teammates with his drive to win. One friend said he played on sheer guts. Sophomore year also proved to be his best scholastically. He managed to finish Latin with a 75; his highest grade was in English, an 81. His teacher said he wrote a "splendid exam," except for his horrendous misspellings, including "Attemp, jelousy, comming, and sieze."

If it was a good year for Jack, it was an outstanding year for Joe Jr., who was graduating. Everything that his brother had worked for since his poor beginning at Choate culminated in the smashing success of his final year. It was probably a first in the history of the school that a Catholic boy had achieved such heights. The most important event at Choate was the annual Prize Day, when graduating sixth formers were honored. One rainy day in May 1933, it was Joe's class' Prize Day, and Mr. and Mrs. Kennedy came up to be a part of it—one of the few visits they ever made to the school.

There were a number of prizes to be awarded: for academic excellence, public speaking, athletics. The most coveted of all was the Harvard

Trophy. The small bronze statue of a football player in a running pose, the ball tucked under his arm, had been donated to Choate by the prestigious university for which it was named. It was awarded to the boy in the senior class who best combined scholarship and sportsmanship. On that drizzly afternoon, Joseph Kennedy Jr. walked up to the podium and, as the audience applauded wildly, accepted the Harvard Trophy.

Jack and Lem were in the audience that day, too. Years later, Lem described the scene in great detail to a biographer. As Lem glanced over at his friend, he noticed that Jack was not watching his brother. His eyes were on his father, whose face was glowing with pride. Mr. Kennedy was applauding so hard, Lem said, it seemed as if his hands might break.

After the ceremony, Jack wanted to get away from the milling crowd, away from his family. He and Lem stomped through the muddy campus until they found a quiet place under a tree where they could sit and talk.

"I know I'm smarter than Joe," Jack confessed to Lem, "but no one understands that. Especially not my parents."

His intelligence, Jack told Lem, was not like Joe's, it was better. Sure, Joe could spit back anything a teacher gave him to memorize, but so

The camera catches Jack and Joe Jr. in an unguarded moment, as the second son intently observes his older brother.

what? He himself had a creative brain, the kind that was interested in ideas, not just facts. He enjoyed reading about things, thinking about them, and making connections to other ideas. It was the kind of intelligence that didn't necessarily show up on tests, Jack argued.

Jack even thought he was a better athlete than Joe. Joe worked hard to develop his athletic ability, but Jack felt he was quicker and more coordinated. If Jack had health on his side, the way Joe did, who knew what athletic heights he might attain?

While Jack poured out his heart to Lem, his parents were strolling around the campus, accepting congratulations from the Choate faculty on what a fine son they had raised. Soon afterward, Mr. Kennedy wrote a letter to Joe Jr. expressing just how proud he and Mrs. Kennedy were of their eldest son, praising his accomplishments at Choate and predicting great success at Harvard, the university Joe would enter after spending a year abroad. Harvard, of course, was Mr. Kennedy's alma mater, the school he had been determined his sons would attend all along.

Later that year, Mr. Kennedy wrote a letter to Headmaster St. John that struck a very different tone. It was about Jack: ". . . the work he wants to do he does exceptionally well, but he seems to lack entirely a sense of responsibility, and that to my way of thinking must be developed in him very quickly, or else I am very fearful of the results. . . . He has too many fundamentally good qualities not to feel that once he got on the right track he would be a really worthwhile citizen. . . . I would very much like to have Jack follow in [Joe's] footsteps."

However, Jack, who already sported a happy-go-lucky veneer when he arrived at Choate, was clearly determined not to follow in his brother's footsteps. As his high school career progressed, when it came to dealing with the school's rules and standards, it almost seemed as if Jack asked himself, "What would Joe do?" and then cheerfully did the opposite.

It must have been a great relief for Jack that Joe was finally graduating. Though the boys hadn't seen a lot of each other on campus, Joe's presence as one of the school's outstanding students was everywhere. Sometimes he would turn up to give his younger brother a pep talk about his grades or a lecture about his attitude. The advice didn't seem to be offered with brotherly affection. Lem described Joe's usual tone as "needling." Jack tried to act nonchalant about these visits, but at least once he lost his temper. Lem remembered the incident clearly. "He jumped up from the bed where he had been sitting—and he was blazing. And Joe grabbed him. Joe was enormously strong. . . . Jack was wiry and not too well and simply no match for him. Joe stood there and held him and smiled that somewhat crooked smile he had, while Jack flailed around but couldn't really do anything."

After a few parting digs, Joe finally left the room. Jack sank back down on the edge of his bed and out of sheer frustration started to cry.

"AN INNER EYE"

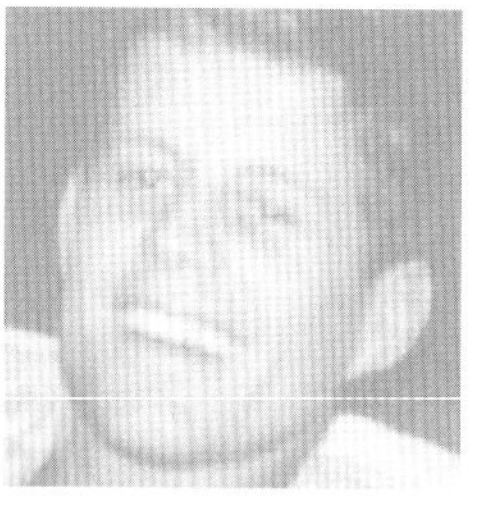

CHAPTER XI

In the fall of 1933, Jack returned to Choate as a fifth former, or junior. With Joe's presence no longer casting its long shadow, Jack had a chance to settle down, make good grades, and straighten up his room and his life. He and Lem had decided to room together, and they were assigned to a dorm called West Wing. If Jack had liked Cap Leinbach and found Eugene Musser a pushover, he was about to meet a very different sort of housemaster in the person of J. J. Maher, the strictest disciplinarian at Choate.

Mr. Maher had attended Choate as a scholarship student in the early 1920s. He was devoted to the school, and his hall in the West Wing had a reputation for being the most disciplined of all. But everything that was important to Mr. Maher, especially respect for authority, seemed a joke to Jack Kennedy. Cap had tried to coax Jack into being a better boy. Mr. Maher was prepared to bully him into it.

A perfect example of the way teacher and student butted heads started with a simple chore: Jack had a trunk he wanted to store in the basement, so one evening he and Lem began noisily pushing the trunk down the stairs. Mr. Maher, hearing the racket, marched out of his room.

Didn't they know this was quiet time? Didn't they care that other boys were trying to study? He ordered them to put the trunk back in Jack's room and take it to the basement in the morning.

Jack and Lem obliged. Promptly at 6 A.M. the next day, they started dragging the trunk down the stairs again. When a furious Mr. Maher roared out of his room and demanded to know what the boys thought they were doing making such a racket at dawn, Jack sweetly said, "But Mr. Maher, you told us to take it down in the morning."

It was behavior like this that led Mr. Maher to write gloomy reports home about Jack. He was horrified that Jack ignored appeals to school spirit and bemoaned his lack of respect for other students—"even to the pleas of not walking on the other fellow's feet."

Mr. Kennedy was equally concerned. After a visit with Jack in November of 1933, he wrote to Headmaster St. John to express his disappointment with the way Jack was turning out: "The happy-go-lucky manner with a degree of indifference that he shows towards the things that he has no interest in does not portend well for his future development." Why, Mr. Kennedy must have pondered, was Jack unwilling to put in so little effort when his future was at stake?

Mr. St. John shared the letter with Jack, who admitted his father had been "rather peeved" during their visit. Somehow, Jack impressed the headmaster enough during their meeting for Mr. St. John to write Mr. Kennedy that "Jack has a clever, individualist mind. It's a harder mind to put into harness than Joe's, harder for Jack himself to put into harness. When he learns the right place for humor and learns to use his individual way of looking at things as an asset instead of a handicap, his natural gift of an individual outlook and witty expression are going to help him."

Mr. St. John's vote of confidence was another chance for Jack to turn himself around. There was a part of him that would have liked to try. Now and then, he'd write his father about how much he wanted to make a fresh start, saying things like "I really feel, now that I think it over, that I have been bluffing myself about how much real work I have been doing." Yet somehow, the promised transformation never happened. Jack's habits were ingrained, and he couldn't seem to change them even when he wanted to.

Instead he got into more squabbles with Mr. Maher, who was insistent that his boys be neat and punctual, two of Jack's most obvious failings. Another teacher observed that Mr. Maher "got to the point where he didn't like Jack Kennedy. . . . It was not a happy relationship."

But then something happened during the winter term that pushed Jack's wrangling with Mr. Maher into the background. Jack got sick again, and this time his illness was life threatening.

He had returned to Choate from his Christmas vacation feeling poorly and looking worse. His first stop was the now familiar infirmary. For a while he seemed to be recovering. Then, in February, Jack fell suddenly, desperately ill. He was near collapse, with a fever and a plunging white-blood-cell count that left him unable to fight off the infection raging through his body. Jack's condition was more than the infirmary could handle. He was rushed to the closest hospital, in New Haven, Connecticut. Despite many tests, the doctors couldn't make a clear diagnosis. They thought it might be hepatitis, a disease of the liver. An even more alarming diagnosis was leukemia, a cancer of the blood, which at the time was always fatal.

As an adult, Jack was diagnosed with a serious ailment called Addison's disease, in which the adrenal glands lose their ability to produce important hormones. Its symptoms include general weakness, loss of weight, nausea, and, at its most extreme, failure of the circulatory system. Eventually the body is not able to fight infections and stress-related illnesses. It's likely that some of Jack's chronic health issues were early signs of Addison's—certainly many of his symptoms sound like those caused by the disease. At the time Jack attended Choate, however, little was known about Addison's, and it was often misdiagnosed. In the late 1930s, drugs became available that kept the disease under control, and once Jack was properly diagnosed, these medicines probably helped save his life.

Everyone at Choate was worried about Jack during this terrifying episode, including Mr. Maher. Special prayers were said at the school chapel for his recovery. After a month in the hospital, finally, slowly, Jack began to get better. But as Lem later remembered, "He came very close to dying."

Through it all, Jack never lost his sense of humor. Red, itchy hives were an especially annoying part of his illness. Told that the doctors were pleased because the hives showed that his disease was moving from the inside out, Jack, covered with bumps, sarcastically replied, "Gee! The doctors must be having a happy day today." After days on a liquid diet, he was at last allowed solid food. He ruefully informed the headmaster's wife, Mrs. St. John, who had come to visit him, "It was just as well they decided to give me breakfast; if they hadn't, I think the nurse would have come in, looked in my bed and wouldn't be able to see me at all!"

Jack was very fond of Mrs. St. John; she was motherly to him in a way his own mother was not. His father came to New Haven to see him, but

If a picture of Jack had been taken every time he was sick, they would have filled several photo albums. This, however, is the only available picture of him in a familiar pose.

apparently Rose did not make the trip. Perhaps she was on one of her faraway travels. In any case, it was left to Mrs. St. John to make sure that Jack had his record player and books in the hospital, and *The New York Times,* which he subscribed to and read cover to cover.

By spring break, Jack was well enough to travel, so he went down to Palm Beach to recuperate and spend Easter with his family. From there he sent Mrs. St. John a very nice letter thanking her for all the kindnesses she had showed him when he was in the hospital. "I'll never be able to repay them, so I'll have to be satisfied with letting you know my appreciation."

After Easter vacation, Jack returned to Choate, but he sorely missed the sunshine of Palm Beach. "The weather has been awful up here, rain every day," he wrote his father. There was something else as dreary as the weather. "Mr. Maher has come back from his holidays looking blacker than ever."

For his part, Mr. Maher, who seemed to feel he was on the losing side of an ongoing battle of wills, wrote in a report, "To say that I understand Jack is more of a hope than a statement of fact."

Jack and his younger brothers, Bobby and Teddy, enjoying the sun in Palm Beach

Jack's junior year ended with an unpleasant surprise. Though Jack and Lem were given permission to room together the following semester, the boys were once again assigned to the West Wing—and this time they were to live in the room next door to Mr. Maher, where he could keep an even closer eye on them. Despite that gloomy prospect for the fall, Jack had a wonderful summer planned. He would spend his whole vacation in Hyannis Port, and he invited Lem along to join in the good times.

But the summer had hardly begun when Jack got sick once more. He developed a new ailment, or rather, a severe recurrence of an old one: the stomach trouble that had plagued him on and off since he was a child. Mr. and Mrs. Kennedy had been told by Jack's doctors that his chances of recovery from his last illness had been only about five in one hundred. Now here he was sick again. Jack's parents realized something more would have to be done. They decided to send Jack to the highly regarded Mayo Clinic in Rochester, Minnesota, in the hope of finally finding out what was wrong with him.

It particularly galled Jack that while he was to be poked and prodded in Minnesota, Lem was invited to stay in Hyannis Port, sailing, swimming, and lounging on the beach. Students then and now feel summer equals freedom, and Jack was no exception. This was a chance to spend time without badgering masters and suffocating rules. He was especially looking forward to something for which there was little opportunity at school—spending time with girls. Jack, like most guys his age, was very interested in the opposite sex. The boys at Choate only saw girls during sanctioned visits or at school dances; at the Cape, there were plenty of girls to hang out with at the beach or to take on dates to the movies. "Girls really liked Jack," Lem recalled. "I hated to admit it at the time, but it was true." His trip to the Mayo Clinic meant Jack was giving up laughs and liberty for weeks of anguish, physical and mental.

It's easy to imagine how depressed and miserable Jack must have been at the Mayo Clinic. His first letter to Lem said, "it looks now as if I'm not going to get out of here till about 12 days." He called Rochester "a hole" and said that even being back at Choate was preferable to being in the hospital. As with his childhood bout of scarlet fever and his illness at Canterbury, he was once again alone in an unfamiliar place, dependent upon strangers to take care of him and make him better.

True, he was no longer a child, but being a teenager raised its own set of issues. He was seventeen, supposedly in the prime of youth. His whole life was ahead of him. Yet how could he see his future clearly when his vision was clouded by uncertainty and pain?

Unlike the small boy at Boston City Hospital who could not understand what was going on around him, this older Jack was acutely aware of what the doctors were doing. It was more than a matter of not feeling well. The tests Jack had to undergo were invasive and embarrassing. First, enemas flushed out his intestines, then scopes were pushed into his large intestine and down his throat to examine him internally. It began to get even the normally high-spirited Jack down. "I have a gut ache all the time," he complained in a letter to Lem. "God, what a beating I'm taking. I've lost 8lbs and still going down."

Days turned into weeks at the Mayo Clinic. When he wasn't undergoing some medical test, Jack tried to keep his mind off his troubles. He wrote letters to his friends and family. There were ongoing flirtations with the nurses; Jack reported to Lem that they were very "tantalizing" and that they found him attractive as well. "I'm the pet of the hospital," he boasted. He also passed the time, as he so often did when he was stuck in bed, by reading. One family friend who came to visit found him "lying in bed, very pale, which highlighted the freckles across his nose. He was so surrounded by books I could hardly see him."

After all the time Jack put in at the Mayo Clinic and all the miserable tests he endured, the conclusion the doctors came to was this: They didn't know what was wrong with Jack Kennedy.

Jack returned to Hyannis Port, a month of his vacation gone, but relieved and happy to be home. He surprised everyone by suddenly feeling better. No one knew why his health had improved, any more than they understood why it had grown worse. One thing was clear, however: Jack's battle with sickness was a defining element of his personality and, in a larger sense, of his whole life.

During his years at Choate, Jack spent more days in the infirmary than any other student. As an adult, he would continue his struggle with poor health. Besides his Addison's disease, he would seriously hurt his already-weak back playing football. Then, during World War II, he would reinjure it, leading to several surgeries and decades of pain. Many years later his brother Bobby said that Jack's pain amounted to "at least one half the days he spent on this earth. Those who knew him well would know when he was suffering. . . . Those who did not know him well detected nothing."

Yet, just as childhood illnesses had brought him his mother's attention, Jack's later confinements also came with some unexpected advantages. So much time spent as an observer of life rather than a participant allowed him to watch the world around him and develop a sensitivity to what was really happening beneath the surface. Lem called this Jack's "inner eye." Like many teenagers, then and now, Jack was quick to spot people who said one thing and did another. He realized this behavior sometimes described his parents, who revered the idea of family but spent so much time away from their children. His inner eye was the source of much of his ironic wit and under the best of circumstances it enabled him to be touched by the world of ideas.

The days and weeks alone in a sickbed gave Jack a luxury of space and time that permitted him to have his own insights about things and to make his own judgments about what was important, separate and apart from the viewpoints of those closest to him. Unexpectedly, his poor health led him to become himself in a way that might not have been possible had he been healthy.

Being ill so much of the time also forced Jack Kennedy to enjoy life's

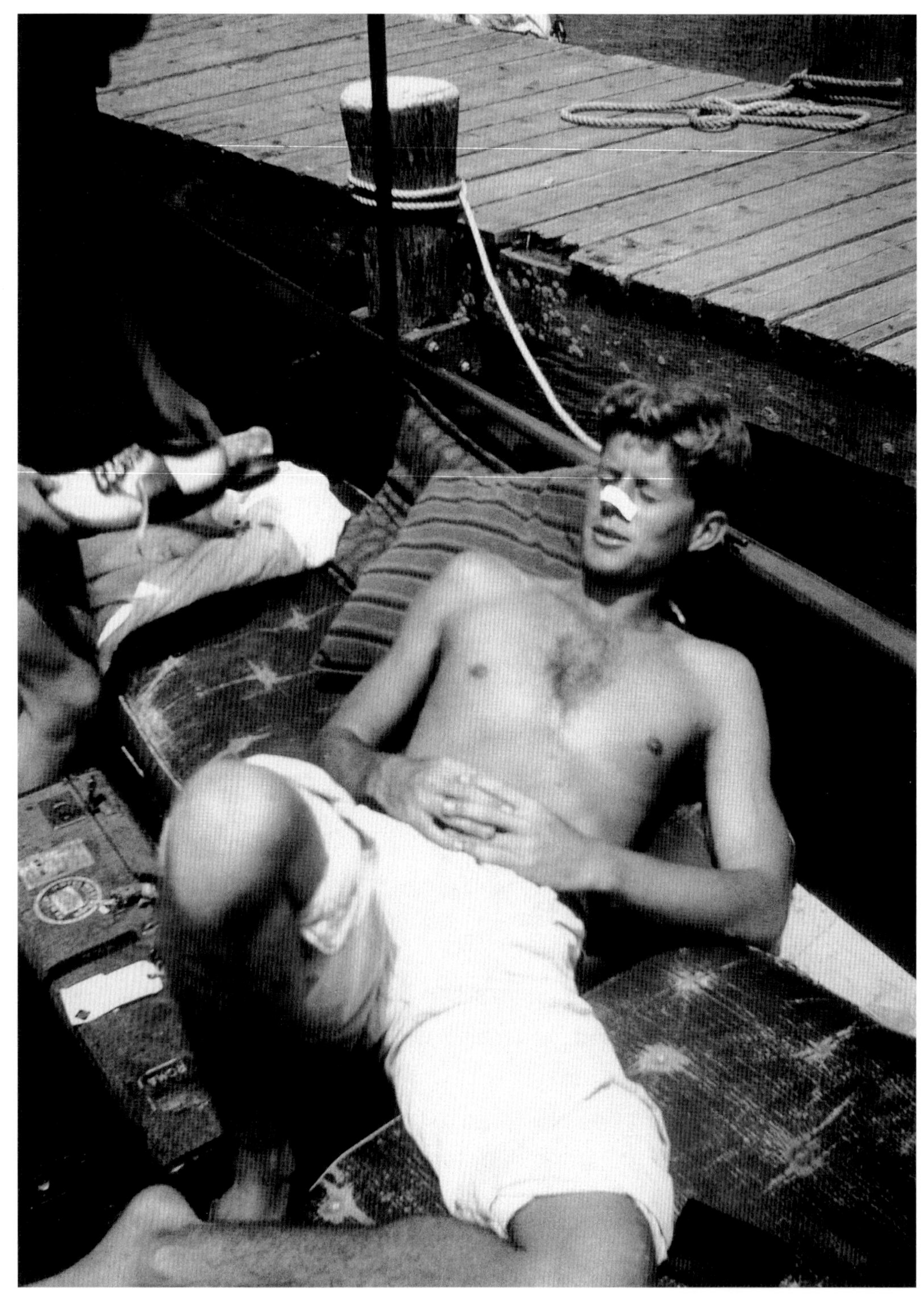

Jack relaxing at Hyannis Port

pleasures to the utmost when he *was* well. Both as a boy and as a man, he played harder, laughed more intensely, and took chances that others did not. One friend vividly described the way Jack lived when he was well: "It's as if he was saying, 'I'm not dead yet.' "

Like many people who experience chronic illness when they are young, Jack realized early that life is not always fair. Mr. Tinker, his fifth-form English teacher, praised Jack's talent for putting his ideas into words (though not for spelling them correctly) and encouraged him to consider a literary career. An essay Jack wrote for Mr. Tinker during the spring term of his junior year shows both the quality of his writing and how, even as a young adult of privilege, he had thought about the inequities of life.

JUSTICE

We read in the news-paper, periodicals . . . we hear from the pulpits, soap-boxes and the other numerous locations that orators choose; about the word justice. Justice is pictured as a lady holding scales in her hand on which is weiged right and wrong. Always is the word linked with God . . . But should this be so? . . . does God render to everyone his just due?

A boy is born in a rich family, brought up in [a] clean environment with an excellent education and good companions, inherits a fool-proof business from his father. . . . Take the other extreme. A boy is born in the slums, of a poor family, has evil companions, no education . . . dies, worthless. . . . Was it because of the ~~poor~~ [rich] boys' abylity that he landed in the lap of luxery or the poor boys fault that he was born in squalor? . . . how much better chance has [the] boy born with a silver spoon in his mouth of being good than the boy who from birth is surrounded by rottenness and filth. This even to the most religious of us can hardly seem a "square deal." Thus one sees that justice is not always received from "The Most Just" so how can we poor mortals ever hope to attain it?

MUCKERS

CHAPTER XII

Jack Kennedy arrived for his senior year at Choate, healthy, handsome, and ready for fun. Friends remember him during that final year with words like "energetic," "friendly," and "forthright." Lem said Jack had the feeling the school was going to be his.

Everything seemed to be in place for a good year. He was finally taking classes he enjoyed. He had come to appreciate Choate's outstanding English department and was one of the stars of his public-speaking class. His history teacher wrote Mr. Kennedy that Jack had one of the best young minds in history he had ever seen. Of course there was that small problem of living right next door to the watchful Mr. Maher. Jack grumbled to his father in a letter that the housemaster seemed to listen in on all the roommates' conversations. "Everything we say he lobs in and adds his comments. We're practically rooming with him . . ."

Mr. Kennedy wrote back that Jack and Lem should try to make their peace with Mr. Maher. But this was not to be. The boys were soon in trouble again. Lem was caught making faces at the teacher; Mr. Maher

A good-looking Jack Kennedy as he neared the end of his Choate years

backed Lem up against a fireplace and shook him until Lem apologized. Meanwhile, Mr. Maher was writing reports about Jack that said his young charge was "matched only by his roommate Billings, in sloppiness and continued lateness. All methods of coercion fail."

Headmaster St. John was still trying to look on the bright side when it came to Jack Kennedy. He wrote to Mr. Kennedy that he was "almost too ready to forgive [Jack] everything when I think of that serious illness he went through."

But those charitable feelings were to change drastically as the school year progressed. Jack was about to embark on a new escapade that would almost get him kicked out of school. It would test the limits of his relationship with his father as well.

By January 1935, Mr. Maher was "getting to the end of his rope," as another teacher put it. Mr. Maher himself said, ". . . for a year and a half, I've tried everything from kissing to kicking Jack into just a few commonly decent points of view and habits of living in community life." Obviously, nothing was working.

What Mr. Maher and Mr. St. John didn't understand was that for them, and rightfully so, the "community" was the whole school. For Jack, community meant his friends, and in that select society he got along exceedingly well. His girlfriend Olive Cawley, a slim, dark-haired girl who came up to Choate for dances, remembered a "witty, clever" Jack who was always surrounded by pals and excitement. "In the group that traveled together, Jack called the shots."

There's no doubt that Jack's "group" had a penchant for finding trouble. As Rip Horton admitted, they fought against structure. "We just liked to bug people and see their reactions." They especially enjoyed seeing how far they could push the school administration.

As the winter term continued, Mr. St. John decided it was time to put Jack Kennedy and his friends on notice that their behavior would no longer be tolerated. Mr. St. John often held assemblies in the stately school chapel. Now he used these assemblies for a series of lectures outlining the proud history of Choate and detailing how to uphold its cherished ideals. As he offered a description of the perfect Choate boy (who probably sounded a lot like Joe Jr.), Mr. St. John also revealed that he had a name for boys who didn't understand the tradition and hard work that went into becoming a true member of the Choate community. He called them "muckers." They were selfish boys, he told the assembled classes, who weren't trying or weren't succeeding or who put their own fun before the good of the school.

Everyone in the assembly knew who Mr. St. John was talking about, even if he didn't name names. But if the headmaster thought his words would end the disruptive behavior of these so-called muckers, he was sadly mistaken. Jack and Lem latched onto the name with glee. Along with eleven other friends, they formed a club, calling themselves the Muckers. Jack said the purpose of the club was to "put over festivities in

Muckers-in-arms: Rip Horton, Lem Billings, Butch Schriber, and Jack Kennedy

our own little way and to buck the system more effectively." They even went to a local jewelry store and had gold pins made in the shape of shovels—since muckers originally referred to laborers who shoveled out dirt and filth. The pins were engraved with the initials CMC—Choate Muckers Club.

Years later various members would remember the club in different ways. Lem didn't think it was so bad. He recalled that the club members spent most of their free time goofing around in the room he and Jack shared, listening to Jack's very fine record player. It was Lem's opinion that the Muckers did nothing more odious than sneak out for milk shakes or play their radio when they weren't supposed to. But Rip Horton remembered his club brothers as "devilish." They planned all sorts of pranks, albeit far-fetched ones. The Muckers thought it might be fun to bring a pile of horse manure to the spring prom and have their picture taken standing in front of it, holding their tiny gold shovels.

The club did just what the boys must have hoped—it drove Headmaster St. John, Mr. Maher, and the rest of the faculty wild. As Mr. St. John said, "I came to the point where I was saying to myself, 'Well, I have two things to do, one to run the school, the other to run Jack Kennedy and his friends.' "

Mr. St. John decided that the Muckers Club was something he could not, would not, tolerate. He held a special assembly and called out the name of each of the thirteen Muckers. These boys, he thundered, were "public enemies" of the school.

Jack phoned his sister Kathleen at her boarding school after the assembly. With high humor, he regaled her with the story of his unmasking. Kick, who had become a great friend of Lem's, sent her brother and Lem a funny telegram that began, "Dear Public Enemies One and Two, All our prayers are with you and the other eleven mucks."

Unfortunately for Jack, Mr. St. John intercepted the telegram. He saw immediately that instead of feeling humiliated by being singled out in the school-wide assembly, Jack clearly thought it was all a big joke. If the headmaster was angry before, now he was furious. He was ready to expel Jack Kennedy and the rest of the Muckers from Choate, ruining their chances to get into Ivy League colleges and dashing their future dreams.

One by one, Mr. St. John called the Muckers into his office. Each now-frightened boy got a dressing-down and was told he would be taken to the train station and sent home by evening. When the departure time came, however, Mr. St. John had calmed down a bit. After consulting with the boys' parents by phone, he gave these graduating seniors one more chance.

There was one parent, however, whom Mr. St. John insisted upon seeing in person: the father of the gang's ringleader. In 1934, Joseph Kennedy had been tapped by President Franklin Roosevelt to head the new Securities and Exchange Commission in Washington, which had been formed to regulate the stock market in response to the '29 crash. President Roosevelt obviously felt that anyone who had made as much money as Mr. Kennedy had in the market would understand its weak spots well

Jack and Kathleen in Palm Beach

enough to fix them. Despite the responsibilities of his job, Mr. Kennedy left Washington on a February day in 1935 for chilly Connecticut to learn just how much trouble his son was in.

After years of shrugging his shoulders when he got into trouble and flashing his devil-may-care smile when confronted by authority, Jack Kennedy was finally scared.

That morning, waiting for his father's arrival, he paced the floor of his room with Lem watching him. Only a few months ago, his father had written him:

> *Now Jack, I don't want to give the impression that I am a nagger, for goodness knows I think that is the worst thing any parent can be, and I also feel that you know if I didn't really feel you had the goods I would be most charitable in my attitude toward your failings. After long experience in sizing up people I definitely know you have the goods and you can go a long way. Now aren't you foolish not to get all there is out of what God has given you and what you can do with it yourself.*

Mr. Kennedy had added that he knew Jack had it in him to be a "worthwhile citizen with good judgment and good understanding." Now, here he was in bigger trouble than he had ever been in before.

Both Jack and Lem had seen Mr. Kennedy get angry, and it could shake a person. He didn't yell or scream. He just stared at the troublemaker with icy blue eyes. In the Kennedy household it was called "Daddy's look," a combination of fury and disappointment, and no one ever wanted to be on the receiving end of it. This time, however, Jack worried that there might be more than "Daddy's look" in his future. His father would put up with a lot of things, Jack knew, but getting kicked out of Choate wasn't one of them. As Lem said, "he was terrified that his father would lose confidence in him once and for all."

Jack was smart enough and finally mature enough to realize that he had backed himself into a corner. He didn't want to be compared with Joe, so he had taken on the role of the indifferent brother, the merry prankster, the boy who never got things done. Publicly he appeared to be happy with that. Yet how did this persona square with what he felt himself in his heart to be: an intelligent and resourceful young man?

The Muckers was supposed to have been an amusing diversion. He had certainly never intended for his life to be defined by the club. Yet if he got expelled, that's precisely what would happen. As a senior, Jack was just starting to form future goals. He was interested in becoming a journalist or a writer, perhaps even the historian that some of his teachers thought he had the talent to be. But to do any of this, Jack knew he was going to have to change his ways. Could he do it? Would he even have the chance?

The three-sided meeting between Jack, his father, and Mr. St. John was not pleasant. When Jack walked into the headmaster's office, his father, already seated in a large black rocking chair, greeted him coolly. Jack later told Lem that he had a lump in his throat when he saw the two men. From the looks on their faces, Jack figured his future at Choate had already been decided.

The headmaster held nothing back. He told Mr. Kennedy everything that had gone on, "chapter and verse." Mr. Kennedy listened carefully; Jack's behavior, he agreed was reprehensible, and he firmly supported the headmaster and the school. Turning to the quavering Jack, Mr. Kennedy lectured him, as he had done numerous times before, about his lack of responsibility. As Mr. St. John remembered it, "He spoke very strongly . . . but he used Irish wit, too. . . . In dealing with Jack you needed a little wit."

After the long, intense meeting, Mr. St. John was finally satisfied. He let Jack off without expulsion. Mr. Kennedy then took his much-relieved son to lunch. There, in the restaurant, he was stern with Jack, but he was warm, too, making it clear that he saw the Muckers affair for what it was, a juvenile prank that had gone too far. To Jack's surprise, Mr. Kennedy told him that the word *muckers* was an ethnic slur against the Irish, a derogatory name for Irish construction workers. Mr. Kennedy wondered if the headmaster had known this while he was using the term so freely.

During lunch, Jack must have reflected on a most irreverent comment his father had made in Mr. St. John's office while the headmaster had been interrupted by a phone call. Mr. Kennedy had turned to Jack and said in a low voice, "If that crazy Muckers club had been mine, it wouldn't have started with an M."

Despite the lightheartedness of this sly remark, Mr. Kennedy was not too quick to let his son off the hook. Looking his son straight in the eye, he said that Jack was very close to losing his respect. Once that happened, Mr. Kennedy cautioned, he would have a hard time ever getting it back.

Jack knew he'd had a close call. The Muckers affair proved a turning point in his life. Rose Kennedy said later, "Something certainly soaked in

THE CHOATE SCHOOL

Report of John F. Kennedy **in** his House

For the Fourth Quarter

I'd like to take the responsibility for Jack's constant lack of natness about his room and person, since he lived with me for two years. But in the matter of neatness, despite a genuine effort on Jack's part, I must confess to falure.

Occasionally we did manage to effect a house cleaning, but it necessitated my "dumping" everything in the room into a pile in the middle of the floor. Jack's room has throughout the year been subject to instant and unannounced inspection - it was the only way to maintain a semblance of neatness, for Jack's room was a club for his friends.

I regard the matter of neatness or lack of it on Jack's part as quite symbolic - aside from the value if has in itself - for he is casual and disorderly in almost all of his organization projects. Jack studies at the last minute, keeps appointments

- over -

Despite all this, Jack has had a thoroughly genuine try at being neat according to his own st,ndards and he has been almost religiously on time throughout the Quarter.

I believe Jack began to sense the fitness of things after his midwinter difficulties, and he has and is trying to be a more socially-minded person.

John J. Maher

This report from Jack's senior year refers to the Muckers affair ("his midwinter difficulties") and indicates Jack's first real effort to conform at Choate.

and deeply." Perhaps it was the simple fact of coming face-to-face with his father's love.

Despite all the aggravation Jack had caused his father, despite all the disappointments, during Jack's worst moment at school, Mr. Kennedy had shown up, ready to do whatever he could to help. Jack told Lem he had accepted coming in second with his father because Mr. Kennedy had always treated him fairly. Now he realized how much his father cared for him, too. Jack understood that whatever challenges he faced in the future, Mr. Kennedy would be there to support him, not just because he was supposed to, but because he wanted to.

As he had promised his father and Mr. St. John, Jack disbanded the Muckers Club. Mr. Kennedy wrote Jack's doctor asking permission for his son to get back into sports, because he thought Jack had too much time on his hands, which led to getting into trouble. Although Jack had played sports from freshman through senior years, his health senior year was not deemed strong enough for competitive athletics. The Kennedys also took Mr. St. John's advice and send Jack to a Columbia University psychologist, Dr. Prescott Lecky, for an evaluation. Jack seems to have been quite

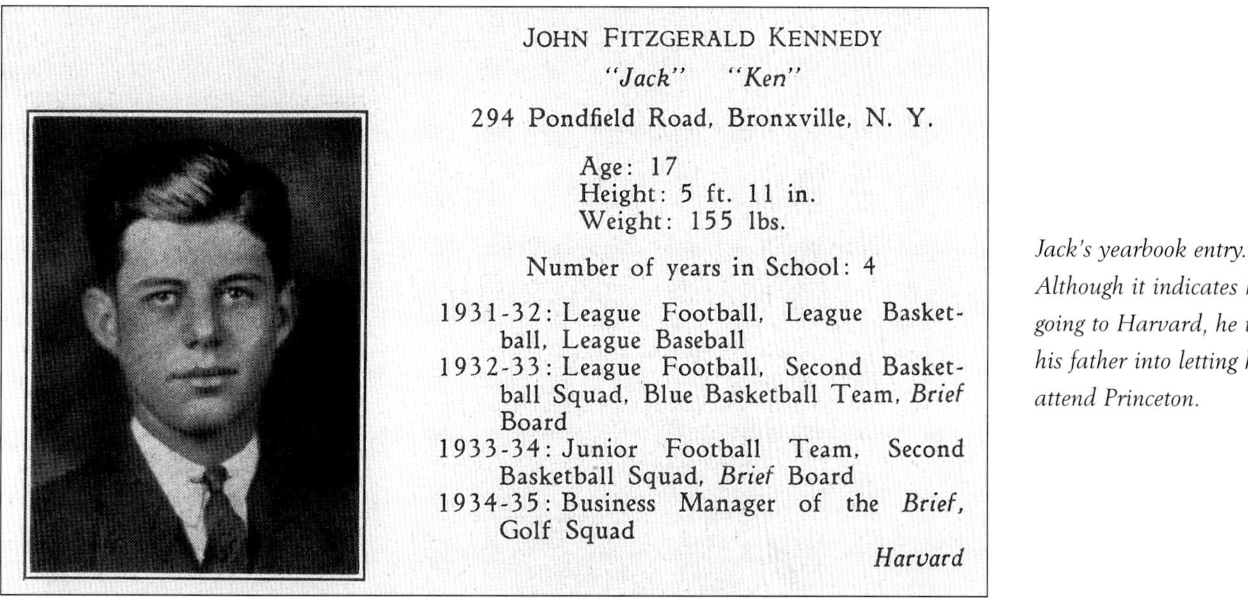

JOHN FITZGERALD KENNEDY

"Jack" *"Ken"*

294 Pondfield Road, Bronxville, N. Y.

Age: 17
Height: 5 ft. 11 in.
Weight: 155 lbs.

Number of years in School: 4

1931-32: League Football, League Basketball, League Baseball
1932-33: League Football, Second Basketball Squad, Blue Basketball Team, *Brief* Board
1933-34: Junior Football Team, Second Basketball Squad, *Brief* Board
1934-35: Business Manager of the *Brief*, Golf Squad

Harvard

Jack's yearbook entry. Although it indicates he is going to Harvard, he talked his father into letting him attend Princeton.

open during their discussions. Dr. Lecky concluded what Jack already realized: that many of this problems stemmed from his competitive relationship with Joe Jr. "He withdraws from the race in order to convince himself that he is not trying."

Now, however, in the final months of his last year at Choate, Jack Kennedy was ready to start trying. "His life took on a new momentum," as his mother put it. He buckled down in his studies, passing his final exams with grades high enough to get him into both Harvard and Princeton. He chose Princeton—the school his brother Joe wasn't going to.

Despite his new commitment to live up to his father's expectations, Jack remained the lively, witty person he had always been. And he had one more trick in him before he graduated. Every year *The Brief* conducted a poll to elect the most handsome, the most athletic, and other leading lights of the graduating class. Jack and his friends campaigned hard, traded votes, and bargained with their classmates until he won the one title he wanted and that he was sure none of the teachers thought he deserved.

It must have seemed like a marvelous joke to Jack Kennedy to see these words printed next to his name in the list of senior class notables: Most Likely to Succeed.

He never guessed they were a promise for the future.

AFTERWORD

After Jack graduated from Choate, he attended Princeton with Lem, but he did not stay for long. Once again, illness forced him to change his plans. By December of his freshman year, 1935, he contracted a liver disease—hepatitis—and dropped out of school to undergo medical tests. Jack spent the following spring on a ranch in Arizona, recuperating. When it was time to return to college in the fall, Jack, who had found Princeton too small and insular for his taste, decided to please his father and join Joe Jr. at Harvard.

In 1938, Mr. Kennedy, who continued to be an ardent supporter of President Franklin Roosevelt, was named by him to be ambassador to Great Britain. Joe Kennedy was a controversial choice because of his Irish roots. Eventually, the whole family joined their father in England, happy to be reunited instead of scattered, as they usually were. Jack and Joe Jr. arrived in the summer of 1938. Joe had graduated from Harvard in June; Jack was taking some time off from school. Both young men worked as aides to their father, sometimes traveling around Europe and reporting back to him about what they had observed.

It was a difficult and dangerous time to be living in England, which was on the brink of war with Hitler's Germany. In 1938, German tanks rolled eastward and annexed Austria and western Czechoslovakia. It was clear to many people that if Hitler and the German army continued to march through Europe, England would be drawn into the conflict. Ambassador Kennedy was in favor of appeasement, which meant he thought England should agree to whatever Germany demanded in order to avoid war. He certainly did not want the United States drawn into a long and bloody conflict. At first, this "isolationist" view had a good deal of support in both England and at home. As Germany became increasingly more aggressive, however, most people changed their minds about appeasement. Ambassador Kennedy did not.

Despite the war clouds that hung over Britain, Jack, Joe Jr., and Kathleen made the most of their experience there. Both brothers had always been close to Kathleen, and now that they were young adults, they were

This formal portrait of the family was taken during Mr. Kennedy's time as ambassador to England.

growing closer to each other. Jack, Joe Jr., and Kathleen were a privileged trio, bright, attractive, and wealthy. As children of the American ambassador, they found themselves in a whirl of parties and other social events. Ambassador Kennedy must have been delighted to see that his children had pushed beyond the barriers of American society and were now welcome in the highest of British social circles, hobnobbing with dukes and duchesses, lords and ladies.

On September 1, 1939, Germany broke an agreement it had with England to stay out of Poland. Two days later, Jack, Joe Jr., and Kathleen sat in the gallery of the House of Commons to hear British Prime Minister Neville Chamberlain announce that "a state of war exists with Germany." Later that month, Rose and the family, except for Jack and Joe Jr., returned to America. The brothers spent their remaining weeks in England helping Americans trying to go home. Jack returned to Harvard later in the fall.

Everyone knew that Joe Jr. was to be the family's politician. However, while in Europe, Jack had become very interested in studying the way political systems such as democracy worked both at home and abroad. He was now considering the idea of becoming a journalist. For his senior thesis, Jack chose a subject he had seen firsthand—England's willingness to make concessions to Hitler in the hope of avoiding war. The well-received paper ensured that Jack would graduate with honors from Harvard. Ambassador Kennedy, always looking for ways to advance his children, used his contacts to turn the paper into a successful book. It was published in 1941 and entitled *Why England Slept*.

Ambassador Kennedy stayed in England, but as his doubts about that country's ability to win the war became common knowledge, he grew increasingly unpopular. He also had little confidence in the United States' readiness for war. By 1941, Ambassador Kennedy was more than willing to leave his post, and President Roosevelt, unhappy with his ambassador's opinions, ordered Joseph Kennedy home.

THE EARLY YEARS

Joe Jr. (left), Kathleen, and Jack on their way to Parliament to hear England declare war on Germany, September 3, 1939.

AFTERWORD

Like most men of their generation, the Kennedy brothers had to put aside their future plans as war drew closer. Jack joined the navy in October; Joe had entered training to become a navy flier in June. On December 7, 1941, the Japanese bombed Pearl Harbor in Hawaii; the next day, the United States declared war on Japan and its ally, Germany. Jack had almost been rejected for military service because of his medical history. But at his son's urging, Mr. Kennedy had pulled some strings, and after several tries, Jack passed his physical. Helping Jack get into the navy must have seemed bitterly ironic to Joe Kennedy. One reason he was so personally opposed to the war was because he feared for his sons' safety in combat. Yet he could not deny Jack's wish to fight for his country alongside many other young Americans.

In April 1943, Jack was sent to the Pacific as commander of a PT (patrol torpedo) boat. These eighty-foot plywood vessels had three engines and were built for speed. Their job was to fire at the larger Japanese destroyers in the area and then move quickly away before the enemy could return fire. In August, Lieutenant Kennedy and his crew of twelve on the PT 109 were out on maneuvers in the Solomon Islands with fourteen other PT boats. It was a night that was filled with confusion. There were Japanese destroyers in the area, and some of the American boats went astray; others did not fire at their targets. One boat was sliced in half by a Japanese destroyer—the PT 109, commanded by Jack Kennedy.

Two crewmen were killed. The eleven others spent the night clinging to the wreckage of their boat and waiting for help that never arrived. At dawn, with their boat sinking, the survivors had no choice but to swim toward several small islands that were likely inhabited by the Japanese. Jack towed one of his badly injured men to safety by clutching the strap of the fellow's life jacket in his teeth and swimming the breaststroke for the five hours it took to reach the island. After a short rest, he plunged into the water again, hoping to find a PT boat on patrol, but to no avail. With little water and only green coconuts for food, the men struggled

THE EARLY YEARS

Jack and Joe Jr. in their naval uniforms. Jack was a PT commander in World War II, Joe a fighter pilot.

against sun, thirst, and injury. When it seemed a nearby larger island might offer a better chance of rescue and fresh water, the sick, weary men swam the three hours it took to get there, with Jack once again towing his injured comrade. Six days after their boat had sunk, two friendly islanders discovered Jack and his crew. He carved a message on a coconut shell with a jackknife and gave it to the men, who led American rescuers to the PT 109 survivors.

This daring story was the stuff of front-page news and magazine articles, and the focus was on the crew member with the best-known name—Jack Kennedy. He received the Navy–Marine Corps medal for heroism. He also suffered through serious back surgery that almost killed him. Years later, when asked by a little boy how he became a hero, Jack flashed his by-then-famous smile and answered, "It was absolutely involuntary. They sank my boat."

Joe Jr. had a distinguished military career, too, flying fifty bombing mis-

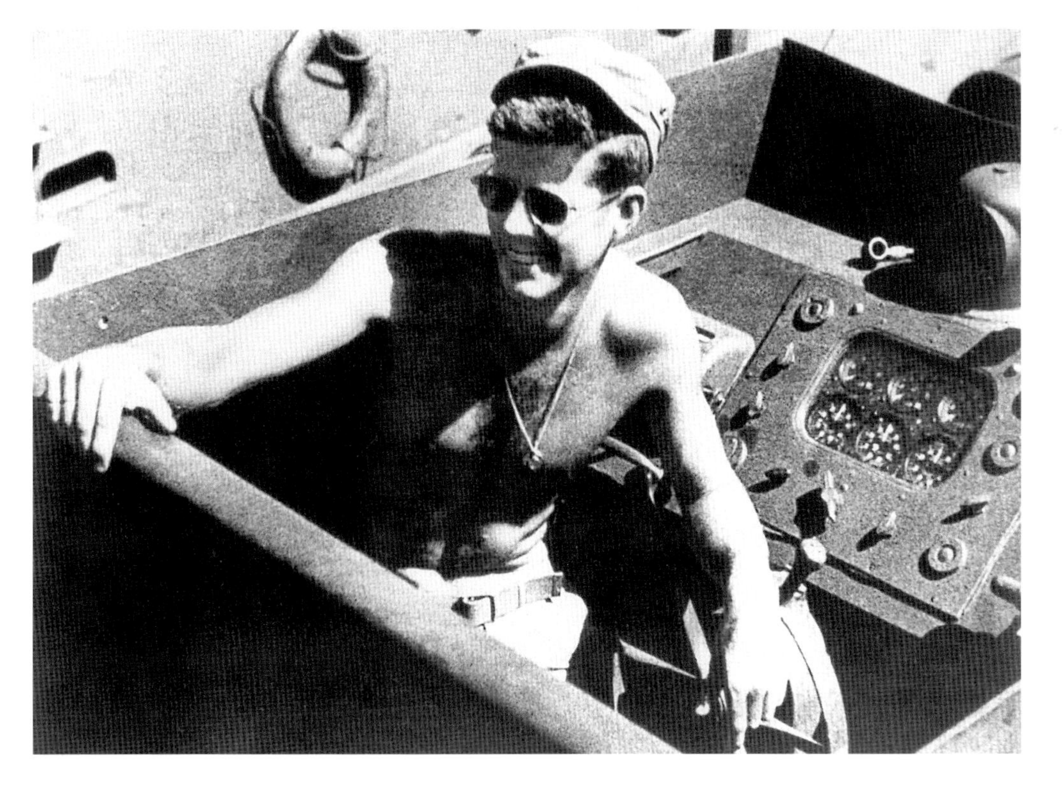

Jack Kennedy at the wheel of the PT 109

sions over Germany from a base in England. But his picture had not been splashed all over the papers the way Jack's was. In August of 1944, Joe was eligible to go home, but he elected to fly one more risky mission.

The Germans had a new type of rocket, the "buzz bomb," which was terrorizing Britain. These bombs were being launched from Nazi bases in occupied Holland and Belgium. Joe volunteered to fly an experimental plane loaded with ten tons of explosives—enough to destroy one of the Nazis' launch sites. The plan called for Joe to take the plane up, switch to an automatic piloting system, and then parachute out. The autopilot would guide the craft to its target, and the plane would explode on impact.

At the last moment, a trusted mechanic told Joe not to fly: the plane's electrical system might malfunction. But Joe went ahead with the mission anyway. Twenty minutes into the flight, the plane exploded. No trace of Joe Kennedy Jr. was ever found.

Why had Joe chosen to make such a dangerous flight? He certainly didn't have to. Was it because Jack, finally, seemed to have bested him? Was he trying for the heroic acclaim that was now Jack's? That is what some biographers think. Perhaps it was simply Joe's faith in his own abilities and enduring luck that propelled him. No one will ever know for sure.

Jack was devastated by Joe's death. How could his vibrant, accomplished brother be dead, and he, the sickly one, the lazy one, the mucker, be alive? He gathered remembrances from those who had known and loved Joe for a small memorial book he entitled *As We Remember Joe*. Jack wrote that "His worldly success was so assured and inevitable that his death seems to have cut the natural order of things."

For Jack, Joe's death not only meant the loss of a brother, it also meant that his own life was going to take a dramatic turn. Mr. Kennedy never got over the death of his beloved namesake. He wrote Headmaster St. John at Choate, "I still can't read about the boy without it affecting me more than I ever thought anything could affect me in this life." Yet he was not ready to give up the dream that his son would become president of the United States. Only now, the son was going to be Jack.

It took some prodding by his father, but after the war was over, twenty-nine-year-old Jack ran for Congress from the Commonwealth of Massachusetts. Once in the U.S. House of Representatives, he grew more comfortable with being a politician and began to see what could be accomplished by playing a role in government. In 1952, he ran for and won a Senate seat. The man he beat was Henry Cabot Lodge Jr., one of the elite Bostonians, a true Yankee blueblood.

There were good times and bad in the years to come. Jack's favorite sister, Kathleen, died in an airplane crash in 1948 after losing her husband in the war. Rosemary began having emotional problems that led to wild bursts of hysteria. Without telling his wife, Mr. Kennedy had doctors perform experimental brain surgery on Rosemary. Instead of calming her as the doctors had hoped, it wiped out her personality. Rosemary was left a shell of a woman, who spent the rest of her life in a small facility, cared for by nuns.

In 1953, Jack married a bright and lovely young woman, Jacqueline Bouvier. Their relationship was strong in many ways, but like his father, Jack was not always a faithful husband. Together Jack and Jackie would have two children they adored, Caroline and John Jr., and lose a third child, Patrick, at birth. Jack also faced down death once more. In 1954, he was operated on again for serious back problems and almost died after complications from the surgery. While he was recovering, assisted by researcher/writer Ted Sorensen, he wrote a book entitled *Profiles in Courage* about men who had taken courageous stands in their political lives. It won a Pulitzer Prize in 1957.

At the 1956 Democratic Convention, Jack was well enough to try to gain his party's nomination for the vice presidency, to run with presidential candidate Adlai Stevenson. Someone else was chosen, but despite that setback, four years later Jack became the Democratic nominee for president.

THE EARLY YEARS

On November 8, 1960, after a fiercely fought race—and helped immeasurably by the money his father put into the campaign—John Fitzgerald Kennedy narrowly defeated his Republican challenger, Richard M. Nixon. Jack was just forty-three years old and the first Catholic president of the United States. Religion was a pivotal issue in the election, but JFK's strong statements about his belief in the absolute separation of church and state in America calmed many voters' fears. The name President Kennedy gave to his administration was the New Frontier. The United States, he felt, was at "a turning point in history." The New Frontier represented "uncharted areas of science and space, unsolved problems of peace and war, unconquered pockets of ignorance and prejudice, unanswered questions of poverty and surplus."

Forty years after the Kennedy administration ended, reviews about its success are mixed. In foreign affairs, the Kennedy administration was marked by disagreements with the communist government of the Soviet Union. The United States and the Soviet Union were in a period of hostile economic and political competition known as the Cold War. During President Kennedy's years in office, the Russians built the Berlin Wall, which prevented East Germans from escaping into non-communist countries. A major failure in the early days of the administration was the American-backed Bay of Pigs invasion, in which Cuban nationals tried to take back their country from Fidel Castro's communistic regime. It failed, in part, because the United States held back its support at the last moment. Soon after, the Soviet Union moved missiles into Cuba, sparking the Cuban Missile Crisis, an event that almost led to nuclear war. The Kennedy administration's prudent moves, both militarily and diplomatically, helped resolve the crisis. In 1963, President Kennedy successfully concluded the Nuclear Test-Ban treaty, a first step in reducing that horrifying threat.

Working with the United States' neighbors in Latin America, the administration established the Alliance for Progress. At home, Civil Rights

During the early 1960s, Americans were enamored of the young, attractive family living in the White House.

legislation was an important part of the domestic agenda, although many activists complained that the administration was slow to make good on its promises and that it was propelled by the Civil Rights movement, rather than being in the forefront of the cause. The Kennedy justice department, headed by Attorney General Robert Kennedy, the president's brother, was vigorous in its support of black students who were trying to integrate schools in the South, like the University of Mississippi.

One of President Kennedy's most enduring legacies is the Peace Corps. During his inauguration speech, he said, "Ask not what your country can do for you; ask what you can do for your country." Americans still are answering his call to volunteer and work with people of developing countries in agricultural, technological, and educational fields.

What many people remember most about President Kennedy's tenure in office is the style, youth, and elegance that he and his wife, Jackie, brought to Washington. Together, they presided over a White House that honored both intellect and creativity. This was especially evident at the formal dinners they hosted in the State Dining Room, where the country's best minds and most talented artists gathered.

A number of the qualities John Kennedy had exhibited as a boy were in evidence in the man who became president. He was still a passionate reader, especially of history; he was often late; he continued to relax most fully on the water; and he never lost the ability to laugh at himself. When asked what flared his continuing back pain he replied, "It depends on the weather—political and otherwise."

President Kennedy was the first president to communicate with the public through regularly scheduled press conferences, broadcast on radio and TV. He held sixty-three televised press conferences in thirty-four months in office, and his wit was frequently on display. Once, when asked about a Republican resolution declaring his administration a failure, he responded wryly, "I'm sure it was passed unanimously."

In December of 1961, during the first year of JFK's administration,

AFTERWORD

President Kennedy enjoying himself at one of his many press conferences

Joseph P. Kennedy suffered a massive stroke that kept him confined to a wheelchair and robbed him of his speech. He lived incapacitated until his death at the age of eighty-one in 1969, a silent witness to the events of the sixties, which would claim two of his sons. Rose Kennedy died in 1995 at the advanced age of 105.

On November 22, 1963, President Kennedy was visiting Dallas, Texas, on a political trip in anticipation of the 1964 presidential election. Dallas, home to a number of right-wing extremists, was not friendly territory for the president, whom many there perceived as too liberal on foreign policy and domestic issues. The Dallas police and the Secret Service were worried. Only weeks before, Adlai Stevenson, U.S. Ambassador to the United Nations under Kennedy, had been in Dallas to give a speech and had faced angry protestors and been hit over the head with a sign. Some officials had even cautioned Kennedy against visiting Dallas. Not everyone was hostile, however, and President Kennedy wanted to be seen by the thousands of people lining the streets, waiting for a glimpse of his motorcade. With the top of his limousine down, he sat beside his wife, smiling and waving happily to the crowd. Policemen on motorcycles rode in front of and behind the presidential car. Two Secret Service agents were in the limo as were the governor of Texas, John Connally, and his wife. Vice President Lyndon Johnson and his wife, Lady Bird, were also in the motorcade. Twice the president stopped and got out—once to shake hands with a group of schoolchildren and then to greet several excited nuns. The motorcade rolled through the Dallas business district, where the crowd was thick and people hung out of windows cheering. Then it headed toward the Trade Mart, where President Kennedy would give a speech to Dallas VIPs.

Now the police and the Secret Service experienced a little relief. The president's passage through the crowded downtown area had been free of incident, and as the motorcade continued, the crowds were lessening. A few minutes from the Trade Mart, the presidential limo passed a textbook warehouse, the Texas School Book Depository. Its employees came out to wave at Jack and Jackie. Mrs. Connally turned and said, "Mr. President, you can't say Dallas doesn't love you." Suddenly, shots rang out. President Kennedy grabbed at his throat and slumped forward, as a horrified Jackie Kennedy looked on. Another bullet found its mark, hitting the president's head, and he fell against his wife, bleeding profusely. The limousine careened out of the motorcade and sped to Parkland Memorial Hospital. Despite their frantic efforts, the doctors there could do nothing for him. Within the hour, he was pronounced dead of a gunshot wound to the brain.

John Fitzgerald Kennedy had been president two years and ten months, about one thousand days.

SOURCE NOTES

Unlike many famous people, John Kennedy never wrote or even spoke much about his growing-up years. Perhaps had he lived longer, he might have put his own recollections on paper. Fortunately, thanks to the John F. Kennedy Library and Museum in Boston, there is a place where researchers can learn about President Kennedy's early years. Many of the family papers, including letters and private papers, are available to look at. There are also oral histories—tape-recorded remembrances—of those who knew or worked with John Kennedy. Although many of those interviews are with people who worked with him during the years he held elective office, some are with those who knew him during his growing-up years.

Lem Billings, President Kennedy's closest friend from his teenage years on, spoke to a number of biographers about his relationship with John Kennedy. With some of them, he shared the correspondence he had received from President Kennedy over the years—he seems to have kept every letter.

Different biographers have come to different conclusions about the relationship between young Jack and the various members of his family. This book contains my own interpretation based on the facts as they are known, but only Jack himself could have told us how he felt about anyone at any particular time. Since feelings and emotions shift and are filtered through time, perhaps not even he could have always been sure.

THE DARE

- The story about Jack and Joe Jr. on their bicycles has been repeated in several biographies of JFK. It is first recorded in *John Kennedy: A Political Profile,* by James MacGregor Burns. Published in 1959, before JFK ran for the presidency, this was the first complete Kennedy biography, and it contained interviews with the then Senator Kennedy.

CHAPTER I: "A VERY, VERY SICK LITTLE BOY"

- Jack's bout with scarlet fever is discussed in depth in Rose Fitzgerald Kennedy's book, *Times to Remember,* in which she calls Jack a "very, very sick little boy." There is also an extensive account of the ordeal in Doris Kearns Goodwin's *The Fitzgeralds and the Kennedys* (where Rose recalls that the house was plunged into a state of "frantic terror" and the quotes from Jack's nurses appear). Shorter accounts are contained in several other books, among them Nigel Hamilton's *JFK: Reckless Youth* and Amanda Smith's *Hostage to Fortune: The Letters of Joseph P. Kennedy,* which also includes a letter from Joseph Kennedy to Jack's doctor about his feelings concerning the illness, along with the payment of the medical bill.

CHAPTER II: "WE WANT WINNERS"

- Information about the Beals Street house comes from the author's trip to Brookline, Massachusetts, where she visited the home known formally as the John F. Kennedy National Historic Site, and from discussion with its staff. There are also descriptions of the house in Rose Kennedy's *Times to Remember*.

- Joseph P. Kennedy's career during World War I is described in many books, among them Laurence Leamer's *The Kennedy Men: 1901–1963*, Ralph Martin's *Seeds of Destruction: Joe Kennedy and His Sons*, and Goodwin's *The Fitzgeralds and the Kennedys*. Original correspondence from that time appears in *Hostage to Fortune: The Letters of Joseph P. Kennedy*, edited by Amanda Smith. Information about Rose's early years as wife and mother appears in numerous volumes, including a rather idealized version in her autobiography, *Times to Remember*, and more layered descriptions in Goodwin's *The Fitzgeralds and the Kennedys* and Laurence Leamer's *The Kennedy Women*.
- The house on Naples and Abbotsford Roads still stands, though it is privately owned.
- Information on the Irish potato famine came from diverse sources, including Susan Campbell Bartoletti's *Black Potatoes: The Story of the Great Irish Famine* and James Donnelly's *The Great Irish Potato Famine*, as well as articles from *The World Book Encyclopedia* (2001) and the *Encyclopaedia Britannica* (1999). How the first Kennedys and Fitzgeralds fared in the New World is recounted in most Kennedy biographies, but especially Judie Mills' *John F. Kennedy*, Leamer's *The Kennedy Men*, and the books of Rose Kennedy, Doris Kearns Goodwin, and James MacGregor Burns.
- The ditty about the Cabots and the Lodges is found on several Internet sites.
- Rose's quote about bringing up children appears in her book, *Times to Remember*.
- It is Rose Kennedy who recounts that her husband said, "We want winners," but in various volumes, JFK's siblings and friends make clear this is the message that they heard Joseph P. Kennedy give to his children. Transcripts of oral histories from JFK's school friends, read by the author at the John F. Kennedy Library and Museum in Boston, reiterate this point.
- JFK's admission that his brother Joe was "pugnacious" and a "bully" during his boyhood appears first in the Burns book, *John Kennedy: A Political Profile*. This point is repeated in every biography through the memories of Jack's siblings, friends, and especially in interviews with JFK's friend Lem Billings. Rose Kennedy also gives a number of examples of sibling rivalries, though she prefers to think that the boys were good friends who shared the usual brotherly squabbles.
- The cake incident appears in Rose Kennedy's *Times to Remember*, as do Jack and Joe Jr.'s pranks.

CHAPTER III: "BETTER TO TAKE IT IN STRIDE"

- Information about life during the 1920s comes from *The 1920s* (America's Decades Series), edited by John F. Wukovits; *The World Book Encyclopedia* (2001); and several Internet sources.
- In *Times to Remember*, Rose Kennedy discusses winter and summer activities during her children's youth and describes the berry picking on Cape Cod.
- Joseph Kennedy's attempt to be admitted to the Cohasset Golf Club is recounted in Goodwin's *The Fitzgeralds and the Kennedys* and is repeated in other books.
- Jack's struggles with poor health appear in every biography, as does the subject of Rosemary's mental retardation. Rose Kennedy discusses her feelings about her daughter's problems at some length, as well as her fears that Jack suffered from lack of attention because of it, in her autobiography. Leamer's *The Kennedy Women* and Goodwin's *The Fitzgeralds and the Kennedys* discuss the topic in detail. It is interesting to note that in the earliest biography of JFK, Burns' *John Kennedy: A Political Profile* (written in 1959), Rosemary's disability is still being disguised. Burns writes that "[Rosemary] was a sweet, rather withdrawn girl, not up to the children's competitive life."

- Rose Kennedy's quote concerning institutionalizing Rosemary versus keeping her at home comes from *Times to Remember*.
- In her autobiography, Rose Kennedy recounts that her husband was the "architect of their lives." She also discusses Joseph Kennedy's interaction with his children, a relationship that is the primary subject of most of the books written about the Kennedys. Particularly insightful information comes from the privately published *The Fruitful Bough: A Tribute to Joseph P. Kennedy*, which was compiled by the surviving Kennedy children in 1965 and is available at the Kennedy Library.
- Mrs. Kennedy's comments about how her trips upset Jack also appear in *Times to Remember*, though she puts rather a good spin on the events. Jack's later admission to a friend that he would cry when she left, until he learned it was better to "take it in stride," comes from Goodwin's interview with Jack's best friend, Lem Billings (in *The Fitzgeralds and the Kennedys*).
- Information about John Fitzgerald and Boston politics comes from Stephen Birmingham's *Real Lace*, Goodwin's *The Fitzgeralds and the Kennedys*, Peter Collier and David Horowitz's *The Kennedys: An American Drama*, and Mills' *John F. Kennedy*, as well as Rose Kennedy's more personal remembrance in *Times to Remember*. Several Internet sources about the Kennedy family were helpful, including *The Boston Globe* 125th Anniversary page. The quote "It's Grandpa" comes from Geoffrey Perret's *Jack: A Life Like No Other*.
- Information on young Joe Jr. comes from Hank Searls' *Lost Prince: Young Joe, the Forgotten Kennedy*, and Collier and Horowitz's *The Kennedys*, where the quote about being the oldest is found.

CHAPTER IV: "WEAVING DAYDREAMS"

- Some of the information about Brookline, Massachusetts, comes from the author's visit.
- Much of the material on Jack's early home life, including his love of books and Rose's discussion of her teaching techniques (such as her bulletin board), comes from her autobiography. Rose also refers there to Mr. Kennedy's not wanting any "monkeyshines or applesauce." Biographers such as Hamilton, Goodwin, and Leamer comment on Rose's discourse in their own books. Other incidents from Jack's boyhood are recounted in family letters, in Charles Kenney's *John F. Kennedy: The Presidential Portfolio*, and in Smith's commentary in *Hostage to Fortune*.
- Eunice calls her brother the family intellectual in Rose Kennedy's *Times to Remember*.
- The anecdote about Jack climbing out the bathroom window is found in Smith's *Hostage to Fortune*. Rose recounts how Jack thought a policeman was chasing him in her diary, reprinted in Smith's *Hostage to Fortune*.
- Rose Kennedy recalls that she often thought Jack was "weaving daydreams" in *Times to Remember*.

CHAPTER V: "A REAL STIGMA"

- The best information about Jack's early schooldays, an underreported period in his life, comes from Hamilton's *JFK: Reckless Youth* and Searls' *Lost Prince: Young Joe, the Forgotten Kennedy*. More information has recently come to light with the publication of Smith's *Hostage to Fortune*.
- Rose Kennedy's comment about wanting her children to mix with those from all classes comes from an interview with Doris Kearns Goodwin (in *The Fitzgeralds and the Kennedys*).
- Jack's comment about being the only Catholic at Dexter was made to his biographer, James MacGregor Burns, in *John Kennedy: A Political Profile*.
- Nigel Hamilton interviewed several of Jack's classmates and teachers at Dexter as well as Myra Fiske,

the headmistress. One of the students noted that being Catholic was "a real stigma."

- Theodore Sorensen, in his book *Kennedy*, recounts the incident of Jack's first "political speech."
- Goodwin's *The Fitzgeralds and the Kennedys* is the primary source for the discussion of Honey Fitz's interest in history. Rose Kennedy also writes with great feeling about her father and his love of Boston history.
- Hamilton relates the incident about Jack and the Rolls-Royce.
- Joseph Kennedy's interest in the boys' sporting life is discussed in most books, and firsthand information, including his pride in his sons, appears in Smith's book of his letters, *Hostage to Fortune*. The telegram to Jack is found there as well as in the posthumous remembrance of Joe Jr., *As We Remember Joe*, edited by JFK, which was privately published and is available at the Kennedy Library.
- The anecdote about the birth of Patricia appears originally in *Times to Remember* and is repeated elsewhere.
- Leamer's *The Kennedy Men*, Martin's *Seeds of Destruction*, Perret's *Jack: A Life Like No Other*, Goodwin's *The Fitzgeralds and the Kennedys*, and Collier and Horowitz's *The Kennedys* all cover Joseph Kennedy's life in business. His personal letters in *Hostage to Fortune* add insight to other discussions.
- Joseph Kennedy's comment about leaving Boston appeared originally in Joe McCarthy's *The Remarkable Kennedys* and is repeated in several biographies.

CHAPTER VI: HYANNIS PORT AND HOLLYWOOD

- The comment about the Kennedy family being a "fish out of water" comes from an interview Leamer did with a neighbor for *The Kennedy Women*.
- All the Kennedy biographies discuss Rose and Joe's relationship. Most agree that Rose strictly followed Catholic doctrine and thought sex should only be for procreation, a tenet Joe did not agree with. Whatever Rose's private thoughts about Joe's indiscretions, she was highly complimentary about him as a husband in her autobiography, though other biographers feel his unfaithfulness bothered her, especially in the early and middle years of their marriage. Additional insights on Joseph Kennedy's affair with Gloria Swanson come from her autobiography, *Swanson on Swanson*.
- In Rose's autobiography, she quotes JFK as saying, "She was the glue that kept the family together," and she notes that though she liked the sentiment, she didn't care for the allusion.
- The quote about the children praising each other comes from an interview done with Doris Kearns Goodwin (in *The Fitzgeralds and the Kennedys*).
- Every biography has some variation of Joseph Kennedy's comment that "we want winners" in the family. Eunice Shriver makes this point in several books, including Leamer's *The Kennedy Women*.
- Some of the information about Hyannis Port comes from the author's visit to the area, including the John F. Kennedy Hyannis Museum. Other information comes from the books of Rose Kennedy, Laurence Leamer, Charles Kenney, Nigel Hamilton, as well as Gail Cameron's *Rose: A Biography of Rose Fitzgerald Kennedy*.
- Honey Fitz's comments on Joe Jr.'s birth appeared originally in the *Boston Post*, July 23, 1915. They are repeated in several biographies.
- Searls in *Lost Prince* recounts the "daring" rescue the Kennedy brothers made of a fellow boater.
- The anecdote about Jack and his boat *Victura* comes from *John Fitzgerald Kennedy: As We Remember Him*, edited by Joan Meyers.
- "Coming in second was just no good" is an oft-repeated statement found in various forms in Kennedy biographies. Here the source is Eunice in Leamer's *The Kennedy Women*.

- The quote about the Kennedy siblings' relationship comes from James MacGregor Burns, excerpted in *John F. Kennedy* (People Who Made History Series), edited by Clarice Swisher.
- The comment about Bobby being terrified by his brothers' fighting appears in Arthur M. Schlesinger, Jr.'s *Robert Kennedy and His Times*.
- The anecdote about the boys and their bathing suits comes from Rose's autobiography, *Times to Remember*.
- The excerpt of Joseph Kennedy's letter to his namesake appears in Smith's *Hostage to Fortune*.
- The cable from Tom Mix appears in several biographies. Joseph Kennedy writes to his son about making a cartoon about Krazy Kat in a letter that appears in Smith's *Hostage to Fortune*.
- Rose discusses the family's view of money in *Times to Remember*.
- "A Plea for a raise" is a document in President Kennedy's pre-presidential papers at the Kennedy Library.

CHAPTER VII: "THE BOY WHO DOESN'T GET THINGS DONE"

- Leamer reports on JFK's shyness with girls in *The Kennedy Men*.
- Discussions of life in Bronxville come from Goodwin's *The Fitzgeralds and the Kennedys,* Hamilton's *JFK: Reckless Youth,* and both of Leamer's books.
- In a Doris Kearns Goodwin interview with Lem Billings (in *The Fitzgeralds and the Kennedys*), Jack is described as using Joe Jr. as "a role model in reverse." The description of Jack as a Pied Piper is Goodwin's.
- Eunice's remark about her brothers being "young gods" is noted in Rose Kennedy's *Times to Remember* and Leamer's *The Kennedy Women*.
- The anecdote about Jean wanting to look like Jack comes from Leamer's *The Kennedy Women*.
- Descriptions of Bobby appear in *Times to Remember* and are repeated in other biographies.
- Descriptions of Kathleen come from Lynne McTaggart's *Kathleen Kennedy: Her Life and Times,* as well as Rose's *Times to Remember* and Leamer's *The Kennedy Women*.
- JFK's description of himself as "the boy who doesn't get things done" was made to a psychologist while he was attending Choate.
- The quote from the Riverdale headmaster about Joe Jr. being one of the best boys there comes from Hamilton's *JFK: Reckless Youth*.
- JFK's letter to his father about Joe Jr. is in the John F. Kennedy pre-presidential papers at the Kennedy Library.
- JFK's comments about boarding school were originally given to James MacGregor Burns but were not used in his book; they appear as a footnote in Hamilton's *JFK: Restless Youth*.

CHAPTER VIII: HOMESICK

- Many of Jack's letters home during his year at Canterbury are in John F. Kennedy's pre-presidential papers, available to researchers at the Kennedy Library. Sections of them appear in various sources, and some appear in their totality in Smith's *Hostage to Fortune: The Letters of Joseph P. Kennedy*.
- Jack reported to James MacGregor Burns that the family's standard of living rose during the Depression.
- In her autobiography, Mrs. Kennedy reports that Jack tried to make others feel he was healthy. Eunice Kennedy Shriver notes the family's position about illness in Leamer's *The Kennedy Women*. The remark about how Rose and her husband felt regarding Jack's health vis-à-vis his grades is made in *Times to Remember*. This is expanded upon in Hamilton's *JFK: Restless Youth*.

- Lem Billings told Goodwin (in *The Fitzgeralds and the Kennedys*) how Jack joked about his medical history, and Bobby's remark appears in several sources, starting with Rose Kennedy's autobiography.

CHAPTER IX: "QUITE DIFFERENT FROM JOE"

- Correspondence between Choate and Mr. and Mrs. Kennedy is part of John F. Kennedy's pre-presidential papers at the Kennedy Library. In a letter to the headmaster at Choate, George St. John, Rose cautions him that Jack is "quite different from Joe."
- Staff assessments of JFK at Choate are in the collection of pre-presidential papers at the Kennedy Library and also in the Choate archives. Many of them are quoted in Hamilton's *JFK: Reckless Youth* and Goodwin's *The Fitzgeralds and the Kennedys*.
- The anecdote about Joe Jr. and the pilot of the *Cape Cod* comes from Hamilton via Leo Damore's *The Cape Cod Years of John F. Kennedy*.
- JFK wrote about his brother after Joe Jr.'s death in the privately published memoir *As We Remember Joe*.
- Joe's letters home from Choate are reproduced in Smith's *Hostage to Fortune*.
- Some details about Choate come from the author's visit there and from her discussions with the staff.
- The quote about the teaching at Choate appears in Goodwin's *The Fitzgeralds and the Kennedys*, via the Choate handbook.
- Mrs. St. John's letter to Rose Kennedy and the anecdote about JFK and his roommate, Godfrey, appear in the Choate archives and are reported in Hamilton's *JFK: Reckless Youth*.
- Joseph Kennedy's chastisement about clothes pressing is in JFK's pre-presidential papers at the Kennedy Library and appears in many sources.
- Much of the information about Jack's years at Choate comes from a privately published book in the Choate archives, *JFK: 50th Reunion of 1000 Days at School*, parts of which Hamilton uses in his book *JFK: Reckless Youth*.
- The quote "Joe did many things well" comes from Jack's piece about his brother in the privately published volume *As We Remember Joe*.
- Excerpts from Joe Jr.'s letters appear in Smith's *Hostage to Fortune*.
- Jack's friend Ralph "Rip" Horton reported on Jack's outstanding memory in an oral history, available at the Kennedy Library. Jack's friend Maury Shea also provides an oral history at the Kennedy Library.
- Mrs. St. John's comments about Jack, as well as her husband's, are from a letter in the Choate archives, reported in Hamilton's *JFK: Reckless Youth*. Comments by Jack's teachers are from the same sources.
- A copy of Jack's request to be godfather to baby Teddy is at the Kennedy Library, part of JFK's pre-presidential papers. The original hangs in the office of Jack's youngest brother, Massachusetts senator Edward Kennedy.
- The incident about Jack stopping home and finding baby Teddy is in Hamilton's *JFK: Reckless Youth*.
- Lem Billings told Nigel Hamilton in an interview that Jack would come home from school and ask, "Which room do I have now?"
- Information about Kathleen and her relationship with Jack comes from McTaggart's *Kathleen Kennedy*.
- The quote about the Kennedy children's response to problems comes from Burns' *John Kennedy: A Political Profile*.
- The incident on the *Normandie* is recalled in Smith's *Hostage to Fortune*.
- Jack's insights about Joe Jr. come from the privately published memoir *As We Remember Joe*.

CHAPTER X: JACK AND LEM

- Jack and Lem's relationship is discussed in every biography of JFK. Billings remained a lifelong friend of Kennedy's, even having his own guest room for his frequent visits to the White House. He kept every letter JFK wrote him, which number in the hundreds, and he shared these with some biographers, especially Nigel Hamilton and Doris Kearns Goodwin. He gave extensive interviews to others, including Peter Collier and David Horowitz.
- A fellow Choate student reported to Nigel Hamilton, quoted in *JFK: Reckless Youth*, that "You never knew what he was going to do next."
- "I think that's what makes two people like each other" is a Billings quote, used in Goodwin's *The Fitzgeralds and the Kennedys*.
- The quote about Jack's inability to "get away with anything in East Cottage" comes from the Choate archives via Hamilton, as do George St. John's complaint that Jack "fostered a gang spirit" and his medical reports.
- JFK's friend Maury Shea said in an oral history that Jack played on sheer guts.
- The description of Joe's Prize Day at Choate appears as an extended anecdote in Goodwin's *The Fitzgeralds and the Kennedys* and was told to her by Lem Billings. It is his words she quotes.
- The author saw the Harvard Trophy on her visit to Choate, where it remains on display.
- Joseph Kennedy's letter to headmaster St. John is among the pre-presidential papers at the Kennedy Library.
- The incident about Joe and Jack's quarrel at Choate appears in Martin's *Seeds of Destruction*.

CHAPTER XI: "AN INNER EYE"

- The story of Jack and Lem and their trunk appears in Hamilton's *JFK: Restless Youth*, as do school reports, which come via the Choate archives.
- Joseph Kennedy's unhappy comments about Jack's "happy-go-lucky" attitude are in a letter to headmaster St. John and appear in Smith's *Hostage to Fortune*, as do Jack's admission that his father was "rather peeved" at him, Mr. St. John's reply, and the comments about Jack's "clever, individualist mind." Jack's letter to his father also appears in *Hostage to Fortune*.
- Headmaster St. John's son, who also became a Choate teacher, recalled to Nigel Hamilton that Mr. Maher didn't like Jack Kennedy.
- JFK's good humor in the face of his illnesses is reported in a number of books. The quotes come from the Choate archives via Hamilton, as does other correspondence to and from the school.
- JFK's quote about Mr. Maher appears in a letter in Smith's *Hostage to Fortune*.
- Lem's comments about Jack and girls were made to Doris Kearns Goodwin (in *The Fitzgeralds and the Kennedys*).
- JFK wrote a number of letters to Lem during his stay at the Mayo Clinic. These letters were shared with Nigel Hamilton and appear in *JFK: Reckless Youth* and are repeated in other books.
- Family friend Kay Halle, in an oral history, recalled how Jack looked surrounded by books at the Mayo Clinic.
- Bobby Kennedy's quote about his brother's stoicism is reported in Sorensen's *Kennedy*.
- Lem's comment about JFK's "inner eye" was made to Doris Kearns Goodwin.
- JFK's paper, "Justice," appears in Smith's *Hostage to Fortune* and is reprinted with the permission of the Kennedy Foundation.

CHAPTER XII: MUCKERS

- Descriptions of Jack, personal and academic, in his senior year come from Hamilton's *JFK: Reckless Youth*.
- The excerpt from Jack's letter about Mr. Maher appears in Smith's *Hostage to Fortune*.
- The letters and reports that flow back and forth between the Kennedys and Choate, and between Jack and his parents, are part of the pre-presidential papers of John F. Kennedy and are housed at the Kennedy Library. Many of them are reproduced in their entirety in Smith's *Hostage to Fortune*.
- The commentary about community comes from Hamilton's *JFK: Reckless Youth*, as do Olive Cawley's comments about JFK.
- Every biography of JFK deals with Jack and his Muckers Club, some briefly, others in great detail. Ralph "Rip" Horton's oral history at the Kennedy Library gives his firsthand insight as a club member. Lem Billings also gave his impressions to Goodwin and Hamilton, among others. Though JFK's gold shovel pin was lost, when JFK's daughter, Caroline, got into a scrape as a teenager, Billings gave her his pin.
- Joseph Kennedy's letter to his son appears in Smith's *Hostage to Fortune*. His quote about the Muckers Club is reported in Goodwin's *The Fitzgeralds and the Kennedys*.
- St. John's comments about the Muckers affair appear in *Hostage to Fortune* and in Meyers' *John Fitzgerald Kennedy: As We Remember Him*.
- Joseph Kennedy's letter to Jack appears in Smith's *Hostage to Fortune*.
- The report of psychologist Dr. Prescott Lecky comes from Hamilton's *JFK: Reckless Youth*.

AFTERWORD

- Information about JFK's time in England comes from Smith's *Hostage to Fortune*; Edward J. Renehan, Jr.'s *The Kennedys at War, 1937–1945*; Goodwin's *The Fitzgeralds and the Kennedys*; and the books of Laurence Leamer and Rose Kennedy.
- Renehan's *The Kennedys at War* is a complete look at the military experiences of both JFK and Joe Jr. Other biographies also cover the events of this period, including the death of Joe Jr.
- JFK's witty comment that he became a hero because "they sank my boat" appears in several biographies.
- Information about JFK's political career comes from various sources, including Mills' *John F. Kennedy*, Sorensen's *Kennedy*, Kenney's *John F. Kennedy: The Presidential Portfolio*, Arthur M. Schlesinger, Jr.'s *A Thousand Days: John F. Kennedy in the White House*, and Swisher's *John F. Kennedy*.
- Information about JFK's assassination appears in all complete biographies. Lee Harvey Oswald, a disaffected loner with ties to both the Soviet Union and anti-Castro groups, was working at the Texas School Book Depository, where his rifle was found after JFK's assassination, on November 22. Oswald was arrested that same day, after shooting a police officer who tried to detain him. On November 24, Oswald was shot and killed by a Dallas nightclub owner, Jack Ruby, while being transferred from his prison cell to an interrogation office. President Lyndon Johnson appointed a commission, headed by Chief Justice Earl Warren, to investigate the events surrounding the death of President Kennedy. The commission came to the conclusion that Oswald was the lone assassin. In decades since, the Warren Commission's findings have been challenged in many books and articles. The debate over who killed President Kennedy continues to this day.

BOOKS

Adler, Bill. *The Kennedy Wit*. New York: Citadel, 1964.

Bartoletti, Susan Campbell. *Black Potatoes: The Story of the Great Irish Famine*. Boston: Houghton Mifflin, 2001.

Burns, James MacGregor. *John Kennedy: A Political Profile*. New York: Harcourt, Brace & Co., 1959.

Cameron, Gail. *Rose: A Biography of Rose Fitzgerald Kennedy*. New York: Putnam, 1971.

Collier, Peter, and David Horowitz. *The Kennedys: An American Drama*. New York: Summit, 1984.

Davis, John H. *The Kennedys: Dynasty and Disaster*. New York: McGraw-Hill, 1984.

Donnelly, James. *The Great Irish Potato Famine*. New York: Sutton, 2001.

Fiske, Lynn. *Choate Rosemary Hall at 100: A Centennial Tour*. Privately printed, 1990.

Goodwin, Doris Kearns. *The Fitzgeralds and the Kennedys*. New York: St. Martin's, 1987.

Hamilton, Nigel. *JFK: Reckless Youth*. New York: Random House, 1992.

Kennedy, Edward M., ed. *The Fruitful Bough: A Tribute to Joseph P. Kennedy*. Privately printed, 1965.

Kennedy, John F., ed. *As We Remember Joe*. Privately printed, 1945.

Kennedy, Rose Fitzgerald. *Times to Remember*. New York: Bantam, 1975.

Kenney, Charles. *John F. Kennedy: The Presidential Portfolio: History As Told Through the Collection of the John F. Kennedy Library and Museum*. Public Affairs, 2000.

Leamer, Laurence. *The Kennedy Men: 1901–1963*. New York: Morrow, 2001.

———. *The Kennedy Women*. New York: Villard, 1994.

Mahoney, Richard D. *Sons & Brothers: The Days of Jack and Bobby Kennedy*. New York: Arcade, 1999.

Martin, Ralph. *Seeds of Destruction: Joe Kennedy and His Sons*. New York: Putnam, 1995.

McCarthy, Joe. *The Remarkable Kennedys*. New York: Popular Library, 1960.

McTaggart, Lynne. *Kathleen Kennedy: Her Life and Times*. New York: Dial, 1983.

Meyers, Joan, ed. *John Fitzgerald Kennedy: As We Remember Him*. New York: Atheneum, 1965.

Mills, Judie. *John F. Kennedy*. New York: Franklin Watts, 1988.

Perret, Geoffrey. *Jack: A Life Like No Other*. New York: Random House, 2001.

Renehan, Edward J., Jr. *The Kennedys at War, 1937–1945*. New York: Doubleday, 2002.

Schlesinger, Arthur M., Jr. *Robert Kennedy and His Times*. Boston: Houghton Mifflin, 1978.

———. *A Thousand Days: John F. Kennedy in the White House*. Boston: Houghton Mifflin, 1965.

Searls, Hank. *Lost Prince: Young Joe, the Forgotten Kennedy*. New York: Ballantine Books, 1969.

Smith, Amanda, ed. *Hostage to Fortune: The Letters of Joseph P. Kennedy*. New York: Viking, 2001.

Sorensen, Theodore. *Kennedy*. New York: Harper & Row, 1965.

Swanson, Gloria. *Swanson on Swanson*. New York: Random House, 1980.

Swisher, Clarice, ed. *John F. Kennedy*. (People Who Made History Series.) San Diego: Greenhaven Press, 2000.

Wukovits, John F. *The 1920s*. (America's Decades Series.) San Diego: Greenhaven Press, 2000.

PERSONAL PAPERS

John F. Kennedy Papers, Personal and Pre-Presidential (John F. Kennedy Library and Museum, Boston, Mass.).

Oral History Series (John F. Kennedy Library, Boston, Mass.).

VIDEO

The Kennedys: The Early Years, 1900–1961. (*The American Experience* Series.) 1992.

INTERNET SOURCES

John Fitzgerald Kennedy Library and Museum: **www.jfklibrary.org**

White House Home Page: **www.whitehouse.gov/history/presidents/jk35.html**

John F. Kennedy National Historic Site: **www.nps.gov/jofi**

American Presidents: Life Portraits: **www.americanpresidents.org**

INDEX

Page numbers in *italics* refer to images.

A

Addison's disease, 120, 125
Adventures of Reddy Fox, The (Burgess), 48
Alliance for Progress, 148
Andrews Society, 98
As We Remember Joe (Kennedy), 146
Austria, 140
aviation, start of, 28–29

B

Bay of Pigs invasion, 148
Belgium, 146
Berlin Wall, 148
Billings, Frederick, Jr. "Josh," 110
Billings, Kirk LeMoyne "Lem," 109–12, *111*, *113*, 115–19, 121, 123–25, 128–32, *131*, 134, 137, 139
Black Tuesday, 91
Boardman, Russell, 99
Boston
  "first families" of, 22–23, 33, 56–57, 147
  historical sites in, 58
  prejudice against Irish Catholics in, 22–23, 33, 54, 56, 62, 63
Boston City Hospital, 8, 124
Boston Tea Party, 58
Breed's Hill, 58
Brief, The, 110, *137*, 138
Bronxville, NY, Kennedy home in, 79–81
Brookline, MA
  Beals Street Kennedy home in, 8, *11*, 12, 13–14, *14*, *15*
  Naples Road Kennedy home in, 17–18, *18*, 62
Brookline Country Club, 62
Buddy (dog), *82*, 89
Bunker Hill, 58
Burgess, Thornton, 47–48

C

Canterbury School, 87, 88–97, 99, 124
Cape Cod, MA, 30–32
Castro, Fidel, 148
Catholics, Catholicism, 106
  divorce and, 65
  Irish as, 20–23 (*see also* Irish)
  Jack as, *49*, 81, 89, 100, 148
  Joseph Jr. and, 89, 114
  Joseph Sr. and, 9–10
  prejudice against, 22–23, 33, 54, 62, 63–64, 68–69, 81, 108, 136
  Rose as, 8, 19–20, 53, 54, 64, 65, 85, 87, 89
Cawley, Olive, 106, 130
Chamberlain, Neville, 141
Choate, 85–87, 96–105, 108–38, 139, 145
Civil Rights movement, 148–50
Cohasset, MA, 32–33
Cohasset Golf Club, 33, 62
Cold War, 148
communism, 148
Conboy, Kico, 7–8, 13, 18, 46, 50
Concord, MA, 58
Connally, John, 152
Cuba, 148
Cuban Missile Crisis, 148
Czechoslovakia, 140

D

Democratic Conventions
  of 1956 and 1960, 147
Democratic party, 64, 68, 69
  Irish Bostonians in, 40
  Jack as presidential candidate of, 147
Devotion, Edward, 43
Devotion School, 43, 53, 54, 99
Dexter School, 54–59, *54*, *60*

E

Ederle, Gertrude, 29
England, 139–42, 146

F

Faneuil Hall, 58
FBO (Film Bookings Office), 61
Fisher, Lawrence, 108
Fiske, Myra, 57–59
Fitzgerald, Agnes, *39*, 45
Fitzgerald, John "Honey Fitz," 38–40, 62, 65
  history loved by, 57–58
  as mayor of Boston, 8, 16, *17*, 23, 40, *41*, 56–57
Fitzgerald, Grandmother, 16, 48
Fitzgerald family, 20, 62

G

General Motors, 108
Germany, 140–41, 143, 146
Germany, East, 148
Godfrey (roommate), 102
Grange, Red, 75
Great Britain, 139–42, 146
Great Depression, 91–92
Guild of St. Apollonia, 9–11

H

Harvard University
  Jack at, 139, 141
  Joseph Jr. at, 116, 138, 139
  Joseph Sr. at, 23, 33, 53, 62, 65, 85, 116
Hitler, Adolf, 140, 141
Holland, 146
Horton, Ralph "Rip," 103, 130, *131*, 132
House of Representatives, 147
Hull, MA, 32
Hyannis, MA, 71, 73, 99
Hyannis Port, MA, Kennedy house

INDEX

at, 32, 68–73, *68*, 81, *82*, 97, 105, 106, 112, 123, 124–25

I

Information Please, 103
integration, 150
Ireland, immigrants from, 20–23
Irish
in Boston Democratic party, 40
prejudice against, 22–23, 33, 54, 56, 62, 63–64, 68–69, 81, 108, 136

J

Japan, 143
Jazz Singer, The, 73
Johnson, Lady Bird, 152
Johnson, Lyndon, 152

K

Kennedy, Caroline, 147, *149*
Kennedy, Edward "Teddy," 70, 83, 105, *122*
Kennedy, Eunice, 30, 32, *32*, *37*, 50, 61, 62, *72*, *82*, 93–94
on Jack, 82–83
as Rosemary's protector, 36, *47*, 70
Kennedy, Jacqueline Bouvier, 147, *149*, 150, 152–53
Kennedy, Jean, 64, 67, 70, *72*, 82–83, 105, 112
Kennedy, John Fitzgerald, Jr., 147, *149*
Kennedy, John Fitzgerald "Jack," *6*, *7*, *19*, *25*, *27*, *29*, 30–32, *32*, *37*, *47*, *55*, 70, *72*, *80*, 108, *111*, *113*, *115*
Addison's disease of, 120, 125
assassination of, 152–53
back problems of, 59, 125, 147, 150
baseball played by, 114
at Canterbury, 87, 88–97, 99, 124
as Catholic, *49*, 81, 89, 100, 148
charm of, 9, *10*, 19, 63–64, 78, 98, 100, 102–3, 130
at Choate, 96, 97–98, 100–105, 108–38, *129*, *137*, 139
clothing of, 88–89, *101*, 102
current events as interest of, 92, 122
as daydreamer, 52, 53
at Devotion, 43, 53, 54, 99
at Dexter, 54–59, *54*, *60*
dogs and, *51*
in England, 139–41, *142*
family move to New York and, 61–62, *61*, 63–64
father's presidential ambitions for, 147
football played by, *54*, 58–59, *60*, 71, 81, 103, 114, 125
girls and, 81, 123 (*see also* Cawley, Olive)
at Harvard, 139, 141
history loved by, 57–58, 84, 128, 150
horses and, *51*
in House of Representatives, 147
in Hyannis Port, 69–71, *82*, 97, 123, 124–25, *126*
ill health of, 18, 33, 43, 46, 48, 59, 75, 79, 91, 92–96, 104, 114, 116, 120–22, *121*, 123–27, 130, 137–38, 139, 143
impact of large family on, 105–6
insufficient attention paid to, 33
intelligence of, 50, 52, 94, 104, 115–16, 119, 125
Joe's death and, 146
larger allowance requested by, 75–78, *76–77*
lateness of, 45–46, 52, 120, 130, 150
marriage of (*see* Kennedy, Jacqueline Bouvier)
memory of, 103
as Most Likely to Succeed, 138
Muckers Club of, 131–36, *131*
in Palm Beach, *95*, 96, 112, *113*, 122, *122*, *133*
perceptiveness of, 125
politics as interest of, 57
popularity of, 81, 110, 130
as president, 148–53, *149*
press conferences of, 150, *151*
pressures and expectations on, 3–4
at Princeton, 139
reading by, 47–50, 71, 150
rebelliousness of, 45, 71, 81, 100, 104–5, 114, 116, 118–20, 130–34
at Riverdale Country School, 63–64, *64*, 79–81, 84–85, *85*, 86
Roaring Twenties boyhood of, 28–29
Rosemary and, 35–36, *35*, 82, 91
and Rose's travels, 38
sailing of, 70–71, 150
scarlet fever suffered by, 5–11, 17, 33, 124
school performance of, 84, *85*, 90–91, 94, 98, 103, 104–5, 114, 119–20, 128
untidiness and inefficiency of, 45–46, 52, 84, 91, 98, 100, 102, 114, 120, 130
wealth and privilege of, 4
wit and humor of, 43–45, *44*, 52, 81–82, 110–12, 119, 121, 125, 130, 132, 135, 150
in World War II, 125, 143–45, *144*, *145*, 146
writing ability of, 127
Kennedy, Joseph P., Jr., 7, *7*, 13, 19, *19*, *25*, *27*, *29*, 32, *32*, *37*, *47*, *55*, 61, 62, 63, 67, *72*, 75, *80*, 96, 105, 112
as Catholic, 89, 114

at Choate, 85–86, 96, 97–99, 114–17, 118
death of, 146
at Dexter, 54–56, *54*, 58–59
in England, 139–41, *142*
father's presidential ambitions for, 69
as favorite child, 12, 24, 40–42, 50, 72–73, 74, 84
football played by, *54*, 58–59, 71, 81, 98
Harvard Trophy won by, 114–15
in Hyannis Port, 70–71, *82*
Jack's relationship with, 3–4, 14, 24–26, 38, 42, 47, 48–50, 70, 71–73, 84, 86, 108, 110, 115–17, *115*, 138, 146
in Palm Beach, *95*
popularity of, 81
at Riverdale Country School, 63–64, 79–81, 85
as role model, 46, 81–82, 83, 116, 131
in World War II, 143, *144*, 145–46
Kennedy, Joseph P., Sr., 8, *16*, *25*, *80*, *82*, 86, 112, 114–15
as ambassador to Great Britain, 139–41, *140*
ambition for children of, 53–54, 59, 69, 147
blackballings of, 23, 33, 62
bootlegging rumors about, 56
business success of, 11, 14–16, 29, 53, 56, 59, 65, 92
business travels of, 61, 74–75
cars of, 13, 18, *29*, 58
as Catholic, 9–10
death of, 152
education and background of, 23, 33, 53, 62, 65, 85
family's importance to, 20, 23, 108, 125
as head of Securities and Exchange Commission, 133–34
infidelities of, 65, 67
Jack and, 116, 121, 130, 133–36
money and, 75–76, 107
in movie business, 61, 67, 73–75, 86–87
in Palm Beach, *95*, 96
as parent, 29–30, 36–38, 50, 106–8
presidential ambitions of, 68–69, 147
Rosemary and, 34, 147
Rose's relationship with, 64–67, *66*
stroke suffered by, 152
wealth of, 29–30
winning emphasized by, 3, 9, 16, 23–24, 35, 68, 71, 93
Kennedy, Kathleen "Kick," 7, 19, *27*, 30, *32*, *37*, *47*, 61, 62, 63, *72*, 81, *82*, 108, *133*
birth of, 7, 8, 11
death of, 147
in England, 140–41, *142*
Jack's relationship with, 70, 83–84, *84*, 106, 132
outgoing, dynamic nature of, 71, 83, *107*
popularity of, 84, 85
Kennedy, Mary, *21*, 23
Kennedy, Patricia, 61, 62, 70, *72*, 82, *82*
Kennedy, Patrick Joseph "P.J.," *21*, 23, *44*, 65, 74
Kennedy, Robert F. "Bobby," 46, 62, 70, *72*, *82*, 94, *113*, *122*, 125
as attorney general, 150
Jack's relationship with, 70, 72, 83, 94
Kennedy, Rose Fitzgerald, *7*, *17*, *47*, *82*, 83, 86, 108, 114, 141
background and education of, 16–17, 65
as Catholic, 8, 19–20, 53, 54, 64, 65, 85, 87, 89
death of, 152
history loved by, 57, 58
Jack and, 45, 73, 78, 97, 98, 104, 121–22, 125, 136–37
Joseph Sr.'s relationship with, 64–67, *66*
Kathleen's birth and, 7, 8
money and, 75–76
in move to New York, 64–65, 67
neatness and punctuality valued by, 45–46, 52
Rosemary and, 33–34, 36
traveling by, 36, 38, *39*, 65, 85
as wife and mother, 17–20, 24, 30–32, 50–52, 65, 67, 94
Kennedy, Rosemary, 7, *7*, 19, 30, *32*, *35*, *37*, *44*, *47*, 61, 62, 63, *72*, *82*, 214
mental retardation of, 33–36, 70, 74, 81, 82, *84*, 91, 108, 147
Kennedy family, 20, 62, 109, *140*
close-knit nature of, 20, 23, 64, 67, 71, 107–8, 125
dinner-table conversations of, 46–47, 107
move to New York of, 61–64, 67, 68
size and character of, 105–7

L

Lecky, Prescott, 137–38
Leinbach, Ernest "Cap," 100–104, 112, 118
Lexington, MA, 58
Lincoln, Abraham, 22, 57
Lindbergh, Charles, 28–29
Lodge, Henry Cabot, Jr., 147

M

Maher, J. J., 118–23, 128–30, 132
Mayo Clinic, 123–24
McKinley, William, 45

INDEX

Mississippi, University of, 150
Mix, Tom, 75
Moore, Edward, *90*, 105
Moore, Mary, 105
Muckers Club, 131–36, *131*
Musser, Eugene, 112–14, 118

N

Nantasket Beach, MA, 32, 33
New Frontier, 148
Nixon, Richard M., 148
Normandie, 108
Noroton Convent of the Sacred Heart, 106
Nuclear Test-Ban Treaty, 148

O

Old North Church, 58
Old South Meeting House, 58

P

Palm Beach, FL, 110
  Kennedy home in, *95*, *96*, 112, *113*, 122
Pearl Harbor, 143
Plymouth Rock, 58
Poland, 141
Princeton University, 138, 139
Profiles in Courage (Kennedy), 147
Prohibition, 56
PT 109, 143–45, *145*
Pulitzer Prize, 147

R

Revere, Paul, 58
Revolutionary War, 58
Riverdale, NY, 62, 63–64, 79
Riverdale Country School, 63–64, *64*, 79–81, 84–85, 86
Roaring Twenties, 28–29
Roosevelt, Franklin D., 129, 133, 141
Rose Elizabeth, 70
Ruth, Babe, 29

S

St. Aiden's Catholic Church, 19, 45, 89
St. John, George, 86, 97–98, 104, 116, 119, 130–33, 135–37, 146
St. John, Mrs., 104, 121–22
Schriber, Butch, *131*
Scott, Sir Walter, 90
Securities and Exchange Commission (SEC), 133–34
Sorensen, Ted, 147
Soviet Union, 148
Special Olympics, *47*
Stevenson, Adlai, 147, 152
stock market crash of 1929, 91
Storrow, James Jackson, III, 57
Swanson, Gloria, 65, 67

T

Taft, William Howard, *41*
Texas School Book Depository, 153
Tinker, Mr., 127

U

United Nations, 152

V

Victura, 70

W

Washington, George, 58, 105
Why England Slept (Kennedy), 141
World War I, 14–15, 28, 100
World War II, 143–46
  Jack in, 125, 143–45, *144*, *145*, 146
  Joe Jr. in, 143, *144*, 145–46

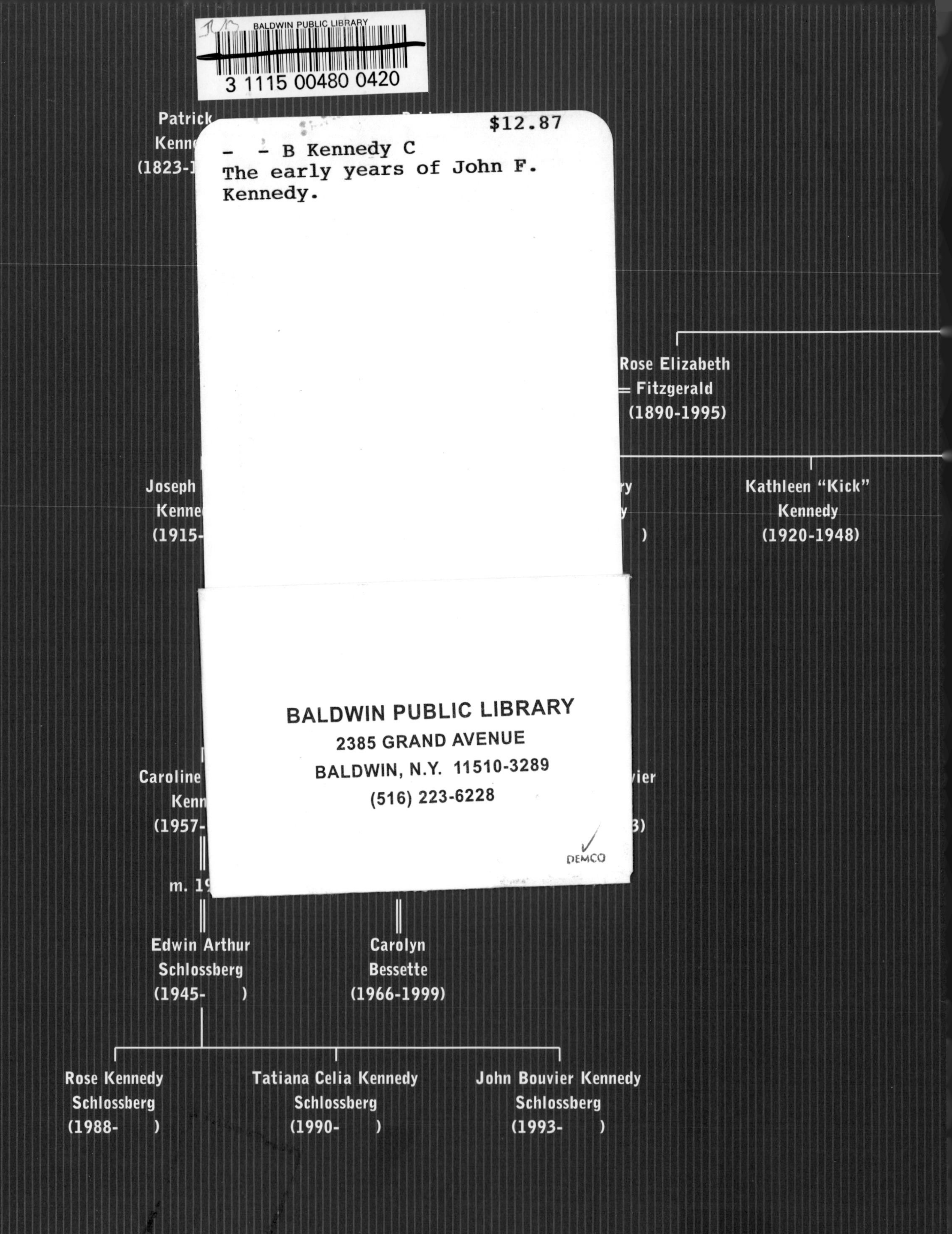

Patrick
Rose Elizabeth
Fitzgerald
(1890-1995)
Joseph
Kathleen "Kick"
Kennedy
(1920-1948)
Caroline
Edwin Arthur
Schlossberg
(1945-)
Carolyn
Bessette
(1966-1999)
Rose Kennedy
Schlossberg
(1988-)
Tatiana Celia Kennedy
Schlossberg
(1990-)
John Bouvier Kennedy
Schlossberg
(1993-)